Arrowheads & Stone Artifacts

Illustration 1
Petrikin Hill arrowhead, Greeley, Colorado.

Arrowheads & Stone Artifacts

A Practical Guide for the Surface Collector and Amateur Archaeologist

C.G.Yeager

PRUETT **P** *PUBLISHING COMPANY*
Boulder, Colorado

Library of Congress Cataloging-in-Publication Data

Yeager, C.G. (Carl Gary), 1942—
    Arrowheads and stone artifacts.

    Bibliography: p.
    Includes index.
    1. Archaeology—Field works.   2. Arrow-heads—
Collectors and collecting.   3. Stone implements—
Collectors and collecting.   I. Title.
CC76.Y43   1986   930.1   85-31179
ISBN 0-87108-709-X (pbk.)

All illustrations and photographs by the author unless otherwise credited, with the following exceptions: Illustration number 112 by Ted DeLeo; Illustration numbers 1, 5, 8, 13, 45, 67, 91, 98, 99, 108, and 110 by Norman Wood.

Cover photo by Ted DeLeo

Printed in the United States of America

First Edition
                5   6   7   8   9

DEDICATION

This book is dedicated to the landowners — farmers, ranchers, and others — throughout this country who are cooperative and generous enough to allow artifact hunting on their property. Without this cooperation, the search for stone artifacts would be impossible for the average citizen, because very few people own enough land to have their own private artifact hunting grounds. In particular, I would like to dedicate this book to those landowners in Colorado and Wyoming who have been kind enough to allow my family and me to hunt artifacts on their property over the years.

Amateur, or avocational, archaeologists have made extraordinarily important contributions to our knowledge of prehistory. In order for them to do so, it is essential that they be able to identify the artifacts which they find, that they keep careful records of their discoveries and that, when they find sites that warrant intensive investigation, they report them to those who maintain state records and who can refer them to well-qualified professionals.

This book should be very helpful for amateurs who truly care about archaeology and who wish to increase their knowledge and to contribute to the preservation and interpretation of remains of prehistoric cultures.

Dr. H.M. Wormington,
Formerly Curator of Archaeology,
Denver Museum of Natural History

CONTENTS

List of Illustrations

Illustration Number:

Illustration 2

The home of J.M.B. Petrikin on "Petrikin's Hill" in Greeley, Colorado, as it looked in 1950. Note the native sod in the area of the Indian campsite. This site is now occupied by the student center of the University of Northern Colorado. *Photo courtesy of the Greeley Municipal Museum.*

PREFACE

A lifelong hobby began for me by accident over thirty years ago on a hill on the edge of Greeley, Colorado. This hill, formerly known as Petrikin's Hill, was then owned and occupied by the late J.M.B. Petrikin, prominent Greeley banker, and was actually rural property on the edge of town near a farm owned by Mr. Petrikin. The hill itself was the highest point in the immediate vicinity, and once many years ago, with the absence of trees, there was, no doubt, a beautiful, panoramic view of the Cache la Poudre River valley to the north and the South Platte River valley to the south and east.

As kids, my sister and I used to play on the hill with Mr. Petrikin's permission. One day, quite unexpectedly, my sister found a perfect Indian arrowhead not too far south of Mr. Petrikin's home on an area of native soil left undisturbed, and probably, the same as it looked hundreds of years ago. Even at a very young age there was no question as to what had been found, and the exhilaration I felt even then was indescribable. My curiosity got the best of me, and it wasn't long until I was visiting with Mr. Petrikin about the arrowhead. I found out that many arrowheads had been found in the past when a basement was dug under Mr. Petrikin's home on the top of the hill. Mr. Petrikin explained to me that many years ago, an ancient Indian camp was located on the top of the hill right where I stood talking to him! From that day on my interest in archaeology grew steadily — all resulting from that one small arrowhead found by my sister in what is now the center of Greeley, Colorado. This arrowhead, still cherished by my sister, is featured on the title page of this book. Petrikin's Hill is now occupied by the student center of the University of Northern Colorado and has no trace whatsoever of its original inhabitants or the ancient campsite.

My thirst for knowledge of stone artifacts has been unquenchable since those early days. A grade school field trip on the South Platte River near Evans, Colorado, led to the next stone artifact, which again was found quite by accident. Later on, my grandfather, Earl Worden, took me to a ridge west of Loveland, Colorado, that is now occupied by a subdivision.

Illustration 3

The author's Folsom point found south of Yuma, Colorado, in 1958, with only a small portion of the base missing. The Folsom is one of the oldest points and is rarely found in most private collections.

There I finally found my first actual arrowhead. A few years later, shortly after I began to drive, a visit with relatives in Yuma, Colorado, led to a side-trip where I found a beautiful arrowhead which I later discovered was a true Folsom point. This Folsom point as I now have it framed is shown in illustration number 3. In the same area, I found five other arrowheads — all in less than ten minutes. This still stands as a personal record for me.

After several years of hunting artifacts in both Colorado and Wyoming, I made my home west of Loveland, Colorado, where my biggest surprise was yet to come. One day while working in my garden, I found part of a white arrowhead. Further searching in the area led to other flint materials and arrowheads, and as it turned out, my acreage contained a former Indian campsite, as shown in illustration number 4. Like so many others, this campsite is located just below a break in a ridge and next to a spring. It wasn't long until my wife and daughter became interested in the artifacts that I had hunted for years. As the months passed, artifact hunting became an interesting and very

Illustration 4
Campsite located at the author's home west of Loveland, Colorado. The site is situated on an east slope and lies below a spring located to the right and above the trees.

worthwhile family hobby — something that seems to be growing and probably will continue to do so in the future. If pursued properly, hunting artifacts can lead to an informative study of the history of mankind and of local history. At the same time, it might just accidently help hold a family together, which in this day and age is an accomplishment in itself.

INTRODUCTION

In writing this book, my approach is to present stone artifact hunting as both a learning experience and as an individual or family hobby. As with any other endeavor, there is both a right way and a wrong way to pursue the desired goal.

The first rule of thumb in hunting stone artifacts is to **always obtain permission** from the proper landowner before embarking on a field trip. Most landowners are quite receptive to this type of activity if a person will simply ask rather than trespass. In some cases, you can safely obtain permission from a person who is simply leasing land. The preferred approach, however, is to get permission from both the lessee and the owner of the property. Gates should always be closed, livestock and property respected, and driving restricted to established roads. Trash and litter should not be scattered, and extreme caution should be taken with cigarettes and the like. In fact, in many areas where I have hunted, there should simply be no smoking at all because of extremely dry grass conditions. Campfires should never be started, and no digging or excavation should be attempted. It is also a good idea to never carry a gun for any reason or to take a dog along. For obvious reasons, the presence of a gun always carries with it understandable apprehension on the part of a landowner, and especially a farmer or rancher. There is simply no reason to carry a gun while hunting artifacts. A small pocketknife is about the only "weapon" that could ever be necessary. On the other hand, dogs can very easily stir up and chase livestock. Such activity can certainly lessen the chances of any return visits in the future.

Prior to hunting stone artifacts, you should know where artifacts cannot be legally hunted or removed. Federal antiquity laws make it a crime to remove stone artifacts from certain federal government lands, such as national parks. State antiquity laws may also make it illegal to remove stone artifacts from certain state lands. When hunting on land not privately owned, check carefully with the proper authorities to see whether hunting and collecting is permissible. Most states also have laws against disturbing or digging in gravesites, which include ancient Indian gravesites as well as any modern grave in an established cemetery. Consequently, in my opinion, excavation of the ground cannot be safely done and should not be done, especially in looking for ancient gravesites. This type of endeavor should be left strictly to the professional archaeologist who knows what he or she is doing and who can obtain the proper governmental authority for site excavation. I do not feel that even the conscientious amateur archaeologist should become involved with excavation. Widespread and reckless excavation by incompetent individuals has always greatly disturbed the professional archaeologist — and rightly so. Pages of the history of mankind can be destroyed forever in a very short time by a careless person with a shovel. In this respect, stone artifact and arrowhead hunting should ordinarily be restricted to surface hunting only.

Chapter 1 discusses what stone artifacts are made of and how to recognize flint material in general. Chapter 2 describes how stone artifacts were made, for this is essential knowledge in understanding what you are looking for and the archaeological significance of what you find. In Chapters 3 and 4, the common arrowhead and specific stone artifacts have been classified to enable you to identify exactly what you have found. Again, unless you know what you have found and understand the archaeological significance of the artifact, the true meaning of artifact hunting is lost, and the value of the hobby is meaningless.

Subsequently, Chapters 5 and 6 explain where and how to hunt for stone artifacts. This knowledge goes hand in hand with what you are looking for, and again, is essential in understanding the archaeological significance of what you are doing. In the final chapter, some ideas are presented regarding what to do with an artifact collection. Primary emphasis has been placed on preserving artifacts in a meaningful manner.

Arrowhead hunting, as you will see, can and should be a very worthwhile individual or family hobby. Even in the day of expensive gasoline, few other activities can be done as cheaply while at the same time providing plenty of exercise, fresh air, and sunshine. Artifact hunting is a wholesome family activity and learning experience that can also be exciting and exhilarating when you find a beautiful arrowhead. Like many other activities, when hunting arrowheads gets "into your blood," even the most advanced medical techniques cannot remove it! Chances are that arrowhead hunting will remain an educational, enjoyable, and exciting lifelong hobby. At the same time, you should always remember that whenever a truly unusual and perhaps quite significant archaeological site is discovered, we owe it to ourselves and to mankind in general to call in the professional archaeologist and not get carried away in a greedy effort to destroy and ravage something with unquestionable historic significance.

I have not attempted to write this book as an archaeological expert — either amateur or professional. I have merely tried to put together a practical guide for the amateur collector of arrowheads and stone artifacts so that he or she will have a better idea of what to do and how to collect in a proper way. I would also hope that this book might bring the professional and amateur archaeologists into closer harmony, patience, and cooperation with one another as they pursue a common goal — the discovery and study of arrowheads and stone artifacts, and the cultures from which they came.

ACKNOWLEDGMENTS

As in most cases of writing a book such as this, it would be impossible to name everyone who contributed, for it would be too easy to overlook someone who should be named. At the same time, I am obligated to identify certain contributors who were essential to the production of the book. I should perhaps begin with the farmers, ranchers, and landowners who make the hunting of artifacts possible through their kindness and generosity.

More specifically, my appreciation goes to the Municipal Museum of Greeley, Colorado, in providing the photograph of the Petrikin home in Greeley. My appreciation also goes to The Stackpole Company of Harrisburg, Pennsylvania, for their permission to reproduce illustration numbers 15, 16, 17, 18, and 19. These well-drawn illustrations were originally found in the *Beginner's Guide to Archaeology* by Louis A. Brennan.

Larry Mades and Bus Tarbox, both in the printing business in Loveland, Colorado, were extremely helpful in the initial stages. They helped me to understand what is involved in the writing, printing, and publication of a book. Professor M.E. McCallum of Colorado State University in Fort Collins, Colorado, was helpful in providing me with geological source materials used in writing the book. William E. Hein, patent attorney of Loveland, Colorado, was very kind in supplying me with the basic concepts of copyright law and procedures involved in obtaining a copyright. In addition, my banker, Norman E. Rarick of The Home State Bank of Loveland, Colorado, provided much needed encouragement as well as a good camera, which I used to take many of the photographs. My brothers-in-law, Kenneth Neighbors and David Sewald, were helpful and patient in teaching me how to use the camera for artifact photography.

Norman Wood, a good friend, did an excellent job with some of the photography found in the book.

I also want to thank my sister, Carolyn Millspaugh, and her husband, Wayne, of Mead, Colorado, for providing the Petrikin Hill arrowhead that was photographed for the title page. My appreciation goes also to Judy Wood for providing me with the arrowhead photographed in illustration number 110. My secretary, Dorothy Manning, was indispensable in the typing and proofreading of the second and final drafts of the manuscript. She was also generous in loaning me artifacts found by her father, Frank Wilkinson, which are the subjects of illustrations 29, 32, 44, 53, 55, 56, 65a, and some of the items in number 104. My artifact hunting companions of twenty years ago, Bruce and Bob Bergstrom, also gave me encouragement and artifact data.

Last, but not least, I want to thank my entire family for their encouragement and patience in tolerating me over the several years it took to complete this book. I want to sincerely thank my wife, Sue Yeager, and daughter, Debbie DeLeo, for their encouragement and also for finding a good majority of the artifacts illustrated herein! Debbie's husband, Ted DeLeo, was also very cooperative in furnishing several of the artifacts photographed for the book. Ted also did an excellent job in taking some of the photographs used in the book. Since I began writing the book, I now have two granddaughters, Nicole and Katie. Nicole, at age four, can already recognize flint and has been on several hunting trips in the last two years. Katie, at age two, is not far behind!

SITE PRESERVATION: A WORD OF CAUTION

The preservation of archaeological sites cannot be emphasized strongly enough. In recent years especially, irresponsible individuals have literally destroyed archaeological sites, in some cases by the use of bulldozers. In almost all instances, such destruction has been illegal and done without any involvement by professional archaeologists. Needless to say, it is this type of activity that has caused much concern by professional archaeologists, legislative bodies, and the public in general. Valuable information can be lost forever even where a well-meaning individual begins shoveling up an area by hand. All excavation of any nature should be done or supervised by professional archaeologists. Excavation by individuals should always be discouraged, even when done upon their own land, if there is any reason to suspect that a true archaeological site is being irreparably disturbed. Indeed, on public land, whether it be federal, state, or local, such activity in most instances is illegal. The arrowhead hunter should, therefore, restrict his or her activity to surface hunting only. In situations where excavation may be appropriate, professional archaeologists should be advised and consulted. We all owe it to our fellow man to preserve such sites for those who follow us. Arrowhead hunting should not become a compulsive and destructive activity. Please, therefore, always consult the professional archaeologist when you have found a site that should perhaps be excavated. Most of our state governments have a state archaeologist on their staff, and most colleges and universities have anthropology or archaeology departments that are quite helpful.

Illustration 5

This photograph contains an assortment of the various flint materials set forth in the illustrations that follow.

CHAPTER 1

WHAT ARTIFACTS ARE MADE OF

It has been said that there is hardly a stone material, or bone material for that matter, than an Indian somewhere and at some time did not use to make an artifact. As a general rule, the Indian used the best material available to make implements and tools. Perhaps some of the more obvious examples are as follows:

(1) Volcanic igneous material such as obsidian is widely found in the Pacific Northwest. Stone artifacts of obsidian are common in Washington and Oregon and relatively scarce in Colorado. In my collection, which includes probably thousands of pieces of flint and flintlike materials from northern Colorado and southern Wyoming, I have but a handful of obsidian pieces. On the other hand, some collections in Oregon and Washington consist, for the most part, of obsidian artifacts.

(2) Igneous material such as felsite is common in Iowa and Missouri and so, therefore, are artifacts made from felsite in those states. However, in Colorado, felsite artifacts are relatively scarce.

(3) Petrified wood, which is more common in southern Colorado, Arizona, and New Mexico than in northeastern Colorado or southeastern Wyoming, is used more commonly in artifacts in the former areas than the latter. An artifact made of petrified wood is a relatively scarce find in my area of Colorado.

(4) My research has indicated that a good portion of the Spanish Diggings material of east-central Wyoming was yellow flint, and, of course, the area is widely known as perhaps the largest quarry of its kind in the United States. Again, artifacts of this material seem to be more common in that part of Wyoming and possibly western Nebraska than in Colorado. In the areas of northern Colorado and southern Wyoming that I have hunted, yellow artifacts seem to be almost as scarce as those made from black obsidian. Some authors have stated that most of the yellow flint found throughout the United States originally came from the famous Spanish Diggings of Wyoming.

(5) Bone artifacts, on the other hand, can be found most anywhere, because the animals from which they came are readily found throughout the United States. If any one type of area has a predominance of bone artifacts, it would more likely be the mountainous regions, such as the Rocky Mountains, since game animals have probably always been more numerous here as opposed to desert regions.

The "Flint" Materials

When hunting artifacts, you generally look for what is loosely termed "flint." I use the term "flint materials" rather loosely throughout this book for lack of a better overall term. What is carelessly identified as "flint" may actually be any one of the following materials: agate, chalcedony, jasper, chert, obsidian, petrified wood, quartz, basalt, or flint itself. An overall view of these materials together can be seen in illustration number 5.

Agate has been described as chaldecony with an irregular and banded appearance. The bands may vary in coloration and be wavy or parallel. As with the flints, cherts, chalcedonies, and jaspers, agate will most often be translucent or opaque. A translucent stone will allow light to pass through it, while an opaque stone will not. You can actually see through a transparent stone such as chalcedony. While I have few artifacts made from agate, they may be easily found in certain parts of the country. (See illustration number 6.)

Chalcedony is sometimes transparent but normally is just translucent. It has been described as a waxy and smooth form of

Illustration 6
Agate.

quartz varying in color from gray to white but can also be black, brown, or blue. Most of the chalcedony artifacts that I have seen are clear to white in color and are quite translucent — some even transparent. Other forms of chalcedony may be reddish brown or red and, in my opinion, would be quite difficult to distinguish from flint, jasper, or chert by anyone other than the experienced geologist. (See illustration number 7.)

Jasper is an opaque quartzite material that is normally brown, red, or yellow or a mixture of these colors, with occasionally a banded appearance. Artifacts of jasper are relatively common and, from my study, it would seem that most red and yellow artifacts are probably jasper. (See illustration number 8.)

Chert has been called an impure form of flint that generally is more brittle than flint. It is usually gray, white, yellow, or brown and, except for the geologist, would be difficult for the average person to differentiate from flint, jasper, or chalcedony. Artifacts

Illustration 7
Chalcedony.

Illustration 8
Jasper.

of chert are commonly found throughout the United States. (See illustration number 9.)

Obsidian is an igneous material and has sometimes been called volcanic glass because it generally looks like glass, especially when broken. It is normally black and very shiny and has sharp edges when broken that can easily cut a person. It is obvious why this material would be suitable for making artifacts with its sharp, cutting edges. Larger pieces of obsidian are opaque, although thin flakes are translucent and many times even transparent. A rougher, duller form of obsidian is called pitchstone, which was also used in making artifacts. Obsidian seems to be more common in the Pacific Northwest, although it can be found throughout the country, perhaps more frequently in mountainous regions where volcanos may have existed. (See illustration number 10.) Basalt is another igneous material that has been used to make artifacts. It is similar to obsidian in color, although it is not nearly as shiny and smooth.

Illustration 9
Chert.

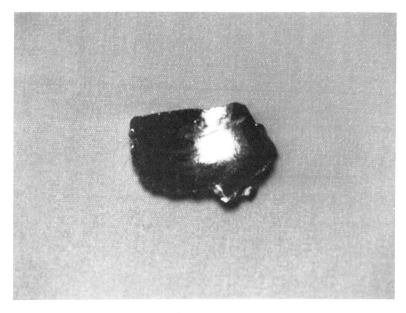

Illustration 10
Obsidian.

Illustration 11
Petrified wood.

Felsite is an igneous rock that has been described as a fine-grained quartz or feldspar. Felsite was commonly used for the manufacture of artifacts, perhaps where flint materials were not readily available. I have seen a number of white felsite artifacts from Missouri but have not personally collected many from the Rocky Mountain area.

Petrified wood is an agatized wood and generally has the flintlike shininess or glitter. Some specimens reveal clearly the grain of the original wood; most petrified wood is colorful and easy to identify. With its quartzlike nature, it was suitable for manufacture into artifacts. Crystals are often found in specimens of petrified wood, further indicating its quartzlike nature. Petrified wood can be almost any color, but most of the artifacts I have seen are generally red, brown, or yellow or a mixture of these colors. (See illustration number 11.)

Although most of the materials discussed here can be generally classified as being in the quartz family, pure quartz artifacts are rare as opposed to artifacts made of flint, jasper, chert, or chalcedony. (See illustration number 12.) Quartz

Illustration 12
Quartz.

Illustration 13
Flint.

Illustration 14
Three pieces of flint showing variations of the typical conchoidal fracture resulting in the cuplike depressions.

artifacts that I have found are white and generally opaque and are delicately made.

I have seen some artifacts made from a sedimentary material such as shale, but on the whole, this type of material was difficult to work and broke easily during manufacture. In my entire collection, I have only one arrowhead made of what appears to be shale. This arrowhead was found in a low-lying area near Cody, Wyoming, and as far as I am concerned, was a rare find.

Flint was perhaps the most common of all the materials discussed for artifact manufacture and was probably more readily found throughout the country. Flint is a member of the quartz family and is usually gray to white, or brown or black in color. It is generally more opaque than chalcedony and somewhat "rougher" in appearance than jasper, chalcedony, or chert. Like the other materials, flint will stand out clearly in an area covered with, for instance, sandstone. On a sunny day in a dirt field, a piece of flint may be visible for thirty feet to the trained eye. (See illustration number 13.) Flint was most suitable for artifact manufacture because of its characteristic conchoidal fracture upon the application of pressure. Conchoidal fracture means that the material breaks in a circular or semicircular manner rather than along a straight line or cleavage plane. Most of the materials discussed in this chapter will fracture conchoidally. The conchoidal fracture is basically a cuplike depression with concentric semicircular lines throughout the depressed area. The trained eye can spot this type of breakage in a rock from a distance of several feet. (See illustration number 14.)

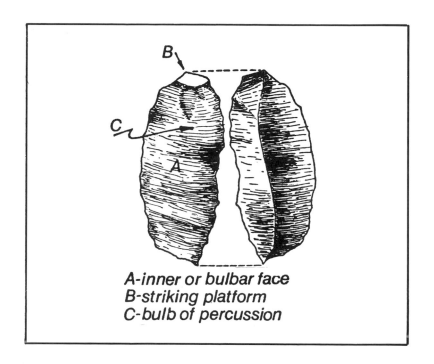

**A-inner or bulbar face
B-striking platform
C-bulb of percussion**

Illustration 15
Man-made flake of flint.
Courtesy Stackpole Company, Harrisburg, Pennsylvania.

CHAPTER 2

HOW ARTIFACTS WERE MADE

In looking for flint materials and stone artifacts, it helps considerably if you have some basic knowledge of how the artifact was made by the flintsmith or native American flintknapper. This helps, of course, in recognizing an artifact as well as the by-product chips and flakes from the making of the artifact. Illustration number 15 gives an indication of how to recognize the manmade flakes of flint in their natural state. A flint material appearing naturally may seem to be just another rock with a smooth outside surface somewhat irregular in shape. Once man has worked the stone, however, as shown in illustration number 16, and has flaked off a chip, the resulting flake, as shown in illustration number 15, is readily identified as being man-made. The inner face designated by the letter "A" in the illustration is usually concave and somewhat smooth and often contains semicircular lines evidencing the characteristic conchoical fracture. Once struck, these flakes provided the basic piece for the arrowhead, knife, or scraper depending upon the size, thickness, and degree of concaveness or curvature.

Generally, three primary methods of working stone were used by the native American flintknapper.

Direct Percussion

The first method, direct percussion, was used primarily,

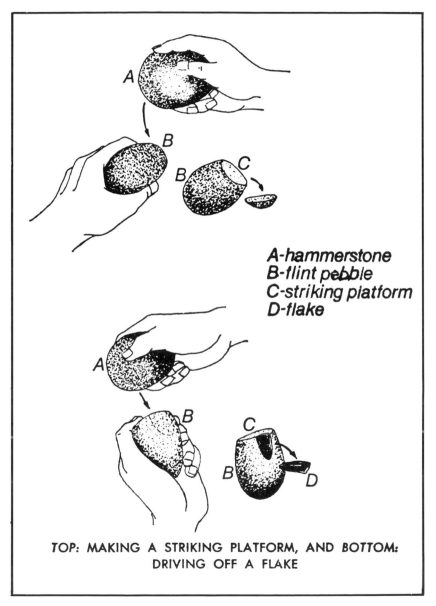

A-hammerstone
B-flint pebble
C-striking platform
D-flake

TOP: MAKING A STRIKING PLATFORM, AND BOTTOM:
DRIVING OFF A FLAKE

Illustration 16
Striking platform for flaking.
Courtesy Stackpole Company, Harrisburg, Pennsylvania.

although not exclusively, to rough out or break down larger flint material into workable smaller pieces. The large piece of native flint was broken down from the size of a softball into perhaps four or five egg-size pieces. This was usually accomplished by directly striking the larger piece with one end of a hammerstone, thereby causing an unnatural or man-made fracture of the core material, sometimes called the mother stone or "mother flint." On occasion, the core itself was held in the hand and hit against a large stone known as a stone anvil, thereby breaking off smaller, more workable pieces known as flakes or spalls. Once in awhile, direct percussion was used in finish or retouching work, but this was the exception rather than the rule. The methods of direct percussion are shown in illustration number 17.

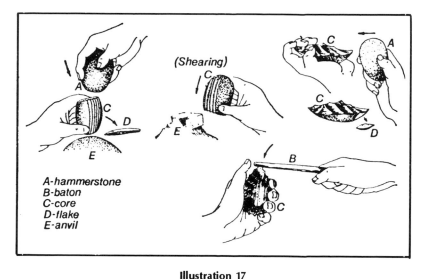

Illustration 17
Methods of direct percussion.
Courtesy Stackpole Company, Harrisburg, Pennsylvania.

Indirect Percussion

Indirect percussion was ordinarily, though not always, used to rough out or shape an artifact to the point where it was readily recognizable as an artifact. Indirect percussion involved striking ·

an intermediate hand-held tool against the core or flake to shape an artifact. The hammerstone was generally used as the striking tool, and antler, bone, or wood was used as the intermediate, hand-held flaking tool. The antler, for example, was hit on the flat end with the hammerstone, thereby forcing the more pointed end into the hand-held core or flake, in turn causing smaller chips or flakes to break off conchoidally from the future artifact. (See illustration number 18.)

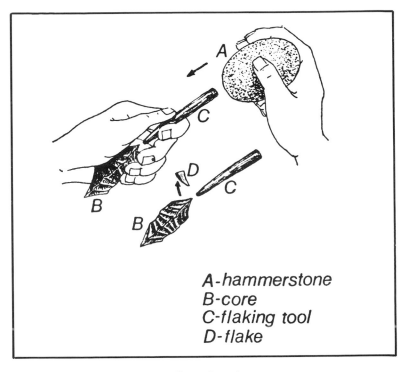

A-hammerstone
B-core
C-flaking tool
D-flake

Illustration 18
Methods of indirect percussion.
Courtesy Stackpole Company, Harrisburg, Pennsylvania.

Pressure Flaking

Pressure flaking was the delicate technique used to retouch or put the final touch or edge on an artifact. Most beautifully worked artifacts were pressure flaked around the edges during construction. In pressure flaking, the antler, bone, or wood tool was pressed firmly against the future artifact, usually along the edges, and at the same time twisted or rotated to one side or another. The tiny flake or chip detached from the underside or face opposite where the pressure was applied. Perhaps the finest example of pressure flaking is the finely "honed" edge of the classical Folsom point shown in illustration number 3. Illustration number 19 shows the methods of pressure flaking that resulted in the finely honed thumb scraper and knife shown in illustration number 20.

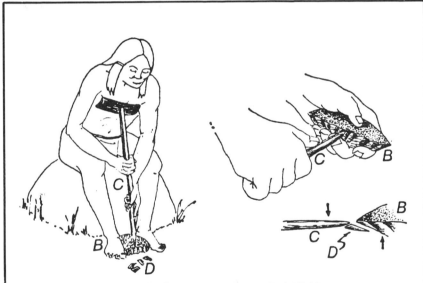

METHODS OF PRESSURE FLAKING

Left: Worker punches blades (D) off the core (B) by leaning his body on long stick with breast rest (C). **Right:** Worker presses pointed tool (C) against surface of stone (B) and twists. Flake (D) is detached from underside of stone.

Illustration 19

Methods of pressure flaking.
Courtesy Stackpole Company, Harrisburg, Pennsylvania.

Illustration 20

Small thumb scraper on the left and small knife on the right, showing the delicate and finely touched workmanship resulting from the pressure-flaking technique.

In recognizing worked flint material, you must remember two basic concepts in stone artifact construction. Bifacial working means that an artifact has been worked or chipped on both sides, while unifacial working indicates that only one side has been worked. Many small- or medium-sized thumb scrapers, such as those shown in illustration numbers 39 and 40, are unifacial in construction. Some stone knives and relatively few arrowheads are unifacial in character; the majority are bifacial. Some scrapers, usually the larger ones, are bifacially worked and are thicker and rougher in appearance than most knives or arrowheads. Usually, but not always, the unworked side of the unifacial artifact is somewhat concave, such as is shown in illustration number 15.

Although it is interesting and challenging to attempt to make an arrowhead by using these flaking techniques, I certainly do not recommend the practice. This was an ancient art and in my opinion should be left that way. Any making of contemporary artifacts only enhances the chance of tainting an historical artifact collection. One exception may be the professional flintknapper who works in conjunction with the professional archaeologist in the study of various cultural flintknapping techniques.

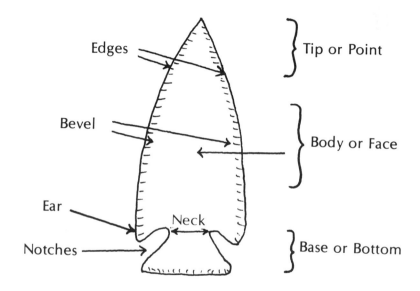

Illustration 21
Basic arrowhead terminology.

CHAPTER 3

The Common Arrowhead

The Indian arrowhead, as it is commonly known, is found in a great variety of sizes, shapes, materials, and colors, depending upon several factors: (1) the type of Indian that made the arrowhead; (2) the area of the country involved; (3) the available material; and (4) the proposed use of the arrowhead. It has been speculated that certain tribes made arrowheads only in certain ways, and from my study, this is generally true. It must be remembered, however, that identical arrowheads could be found in completely different parts of the United States and could have been made by totally separate and unique tribes of Indians hundreds of miles and years apart. Certain types of arrowheads are, however, more commonly found in some parts of the country than in others. The black volcanic obsidian arrowhead, or the so-called gem point made of agate, jasper, and the more colorful stones, is far more common in Oregon and the Pacific Northwest where these materials are found more readily. In northern Colorado, by contrast, obsidian deposits and agate are difficult to find. By the same token, an arrowhead made of white quartz can more likely be found in the northern Colorado mountains than, for example, in Missouri, where quartz is not as common. Conversely, a white-colored felsite arrowhead may be found widely in Missouri and yet be rare in the mountains and foothills of Colorado and Wyoming. Likewise, an arrowhead made of petrified wood would probably be more common in Arizona, New Mexico, or Colorado than in a Great Plains state.

Arrowhead Terminology

In the study and collecting of arrowheads, you should first become familiar with the general arrowhead terminology as shown in illustration number 21. The various parts of an arrowhead consist primarily of the tip or point, the center-section or body, and the bottom or base, including the notches. The bevel is the slope or slant of the surface or face of the arrowhead, while the edge is the surface at each side.

Birdpoint and Spearpoint

The proposed use of an arrowhead will obviously have a bearing on its size. The smaller arrowhead commonly known as the birdpoint was used by the Indian to kill small game such as the rabbit, waterfowl, and birds. It seems unlikely that the Indian would have used the larger spearpoint to kill small game, although it certainly would have been possible. Likewise, the larger arrowhead, or perhaps spearpoint, was probably used to hunt deer, antelope, elk, and buffalo, although the smaller arrowhead or birdpoint could undoubtedly bring down big game if it was shot in the right manner and the animal was struck in the right place. The various arrowhead sizes are shown in illustration number 22, ranging from the three-inch (or more) spearpoint to the half-inch (or less) birdpoint.

Notch Types

Arrowheads are generally classified according to the following notch types: (1) side-notched, (2) bottom-notched, (3) corner-notched, (4) corner-notched and bottom-notched, (5) side-notched and bottom-notched, (6) stemmed and bottom-notched, and (7) notchless, either triangular or oblong in shape—sometimes called "stemmed" or "shouldered." (See illustration number 23.)

Again, certain notch types are more common to some areas than others, and yet on one ridge in the northern Colorado

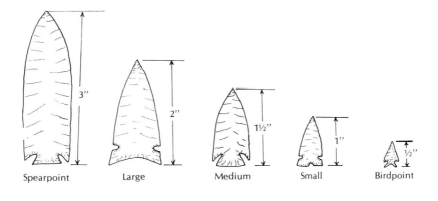

Illustration 22
General arrowhead sizes.

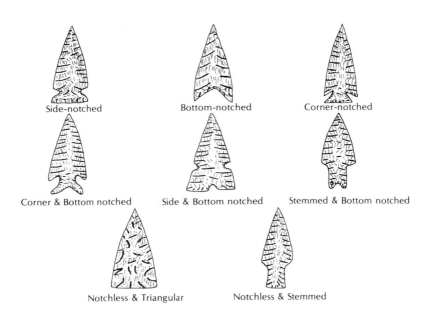

Illustration 23
Typical arrowhead notch and base types.

foothills, all six notch types were found on the surface in a rather limited area. This suggests to me an area that was either heavily inhabited or hunted by a variety of Indian tribes over a period of years, or an area in which a particular Indian tribe lived and made many different types of arrowheads.

Archaeologists, both professional and amateur, have categorized arrowheads over the years based primarily on notch types. It is the notching of an arrowhead along the sides or at the base which gives the arrowhead its individual characteristic and makes it distinguishable from another. Hence, it is much more informative and interesting to find the base of arrowhead, rather than the tip. Obviously, most tips are the same, except for general size, and you cannot determine from the tip what kind of base the arrowhead originally had. It should also be noted that in certain instances, the flaking pattern is also quite important in categorizing a particular projectile point. This is especially true where the overall shape is similar.

Broken Arrowheads

In hunting arrowheads, you should constantly be looking for flint materials with the characteristic shapes of the tip, the center-section, or the base. It is very easy to walk right over or even step on a part of an arrowhead and not even know it! To the untrained eye, the center-section may appear as just another small piece of flint not worth bending over to pick up. The tip and base, of course, are more easily identified as once being part of a larger arrowhead. Various parts of arrowheads are depicted in illustration number 24 in such a manner as to also indicate what the entire arrowhead once looked like before it was broken. You should actually memorize the various base styles, for this is the key to spotting arrowheads or parts of them in the field.

The Stunner

The arrowhead commonly known as the "stunner" is perhaps one of the more puzzling artifacts. It is certainly the exception to the basic proposition that all tips are generally the same. This

Illustration 24

Commonly found pieces of arrowheads.

arrowhead is also called a "bunt" by some authorities. The stunner is not hard to recognize if you have found one. In my experience, the true stunner is rare in northern Colorado and southern Wyoming, and probably most everywhere. You must be careful in classifying an arrowhead as a stunner, because frequently the tip of an arrowhead may be broken in such a manner, giving it the appearance of a stunner. This false appearance usually results from a shattering fracture of the tip rather than a good, clean break. The true stunner on close examination will reveal careful, deliberate, and delicate workmanship into a rounded tip rather than a point. (See illustration number 25.)

The stunner gets its name from speculation that it was shot with a bow and arrow to merely stun or daze an animal, rather than to penetrate or kill. Personally, I think that the stunner also may have been hafted onto a short shaft and used as a gouge or scraper in removing marrow from bones that were too long to be accessible by the hand-held scraper or gouge. This speculation is also grounded on the proposition that I have yet to hear or read of any reason why Indians would have ever wanted to just "stun" an animal—unless, perhaps, they did not want to ruin any of the meat with a penetration wound (which is unlikely, although possible). In addition, some small scrapers have been found which were actually notched for attachment to a shaft. These can usually be distinguished from the stunner because they are normally somewhat thicker than the thin, arrowhead-type of stunner.

True Stunner   Broken Arrowhead

Illustration 25

The true stunner compared with a broken and rounded off arrowhead.

The Serrated Arrowhead

Another type of arrowhead that in my opinion is rarely found in the areas with which I am familiar is the serrated edge point shown in illustration number 26. Although I have seen many pictures of these arrowheads, I can recall very few such points being found in perfect condition in northern Colorado or southern Wyoming in recent years. I have found a few broken serrated points, but the whole serrated point must be extremely rare. Generally, the edge of an arrowhead is one continuous plane from base to tip with no indentations unless chipped or broken. The serrated-edge arrowhead will have many uniform small indentations along each edge in a sawtoothlike pattern. It would seem that such a point would have been very difficult to make and would have required meticulous workmanship. Some authorities believe this artifact was used as a knife rather than an arrowhead. In such cases, it was probably used by hafting onto a shaft rather than simply held in the hand.

Illustration 26

A somewhat exaggerated illustration of the serrated arrowhead showing deep but finely worked serrations on each edge of the point. Many serrated arrowheads have smaller and less obvious serrations on each edge.

The Poison Point

A so-called "poison point" can generally be almost any

arrowhead that was used to not only pierce the hide of an animal, but also to poison the animal. Most poison points were notchless and triangular in shape so that should the shaft of the arrow be jarred loose or fall from the wound in the animal, the arrowhead would detach easily and remain in the wound. In order to poison the animal, an arrowhead would have been previously soaked in rattlesnake venom or baked in decayed meat. Another method of poisoning was to place an arrowhead in an animal's liver, place the liver on an ant hill, and let the liver decay while at the same time being constantly bitten by the ants. Also, some steel arrowheads were allowed to rust and were then baked in decayed meat before use in hunting. The poison point is shown in illustration number 27.

I personally feel that most triangular notchless arrowheads were actually hafted onto an arrow shaft in a firm manner without the help of notches and were simply used in the same manner as any other arrowhead, and not really as the so-called poison point.

Illustration 27
A simple illustration of the common notchless triangular arrowhead, sometimes called a "poison point."

The Quarry Blank

A quarry blank is a rather small or medium-sized, thin, leaf-shaped piece of flint material that can easily be mistaken for a small knife, scraper, or triangular notchless arrowhead. The Indian broke down larger pieces of flint into blades or flakes for easier transportation. These blades or flakes were then worked

Quarry Blank

Stemmed & Bottom Notched

Corner Notched

Side Notched

Bottom Notched & Side Notched

Illustration 28

This illustration shows examples of the various notch types and styles of arrowheads that could result from the same quarry blank.

generally into a leaf-shaped piece that could be easily worked into an arrowhead at some future time. In illustration number 28, the quarry blank is shown in the various ways in which it could be refined and notched into a specific arrowhead.

The Steel Arrowhead

As the white man began intruding into Indian lands, especially when trappers and fur traders began their penetration into the Midwest and West, yet another type of arrowhead came into common usage among the American Indians. This was the steel arrowhead, which was initially traded to the Indians by the intruders. The Indians, no doubt, realized the effectivensss and durability of such an arrowhead. Even today, steel-tipped arrows are widely used in bow hunting. The era of the steel-tipped arrow for the Indians, however, was short-lived because of the introduction of firearms not long after the steel arrowhead was

Illustration 29
Two examples of the typical steel arrowhead used on the western plains in the late 1800s.

first traded to them. It has also been said that the Indian himself learned to make steel arrowheads from scrap metal, such as old barrel hoops left behind by the pioneers moving westward. In any event, a steel arrowhead is a rare find because of the more rapid oxidation or rusting of steel over the years as compared to little, if any, deterioration of stone or the flint-type materials of the classical arrowhead. (See illustration number 29 for the two types of steel arrowhead found by a homesteader years ago in southern Wyoming.)

The Contemporary Arrowhead

Finally, now that the white man has dominated the entire United States for the last one hundred years, the ancient art of "flintknapping" has once again become popular, and another type of arrowhead has begun to appear. This is the contemporary (as opposed to historic or ancient) arrowhead, which in my opinion is common at least in the western United States, primarily in souvenir shops and tourist areas. My definition of a contemporary arrowhead is one that has been made in recent years for the specific purpose of resale to the public as a genuine historic arrowhead. Once you have become familiar with the flintknapping process and the ancient arrowhead, it is generally not difficult to spot these contemporary versions.

Many contemporary arrowheads have been worked on only one side, whereas the historic arrowhead will almost always have been worked on both sides. I have seen some modern-day arrowheads, however, made by an expert flintknapper which were impossible to detect as contemporary. Illustration numbers 30 and 31 show such contemporary arrowheads.

Illustration number 32 has been included to show some of the types of arrowheads and stone artifacts that can still be found today. Those pictured were, for the most part, found on one ranch in southern Wyoming and demonstrate the wide variety of notch types, sizes, and colors of flint materials that can be found in one area. The upper row of artifacts is especially interesting, with a notched scraper on each end (as opposed to stunners) and the crescent, knife, and drill in the center of the row. However, for each perfect artifact, as shown in this illustration, you will

Illustration 30
Three contemporary arrowheads that could be easily mistaken for genuine historic artifacts.

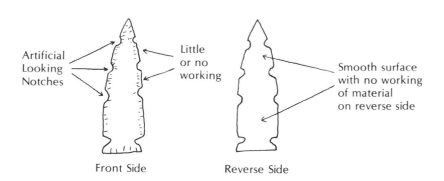

Artificial Looking Notches

Little or no working

Smooth surface with no working of material on reverse side

Front Side   Reverse Side

Illustration 31
The contemporary arrowhead.

generally find eight to ten broken artifacts. Even the broken artifacts may be few and far between in many areas.

Illustration 32

Various assorted arrowheads and artifacts found in southern Wyoming. Note the different types of flint materials and notch types of arrowheads found in the same general location. Also, note the scraper made for hafting onto a shaft in the upper left-hand corner compared with a true stunner in the upper right-hand corner of the photograph. The top row also contains a typical bifacial knife, second from the left, and a unifacial crescent, second from the right, with a somewhat crude drill in the center.

Projectile Point Identification Guide

Illustration number 32a will give you a general idea of the various types of arrowheads and spearpoints found throughout the United States. Many of those shown are quite similar and are hard to differentiate from other points. Often, the same arrowhead may be named differently depending upon the part of the country in which it is found.

Generally, the projectile points illustrated are categorized according to the general age of the artifact into Paleo points, Archaic points, and Woodland points. The older projectile points are Paleo points and are, in most cases, spearpoints rather than arrowheads, having been made and used before the bow and arrow. Much of the finer workmanship is found with Paleo points. Also, the points tend to be larger than those of later time periods.

Archaic points are not as old as Paleo points but are typically older than the Woodland points, which are the newer or more recent arrowheads. Many arrowheads found today as surface finds are hard to classify as either Archaic or Woodland unless, of course, you have found an arrowhead that is obviously a certain named point. Sometimes with the larger arrowheads it is hard to say whether they were used as arrowheads or spearpoints. Speculation, in many cases, simply cannot be avoided.

The projectile points illustrated do not include every point ever found anywhere. However, they do include the most commonly found points in the United States and, more particularly in the western part of the country. On the other hand, many of the points shown are extremely rare and hard to find, especially those shown as Paleo points.

In many cases the flaking technique used on the face of the point or along the edges or base of the point is the primary characteristic used to categorize or classify the artifact. Illustration number 32a does not purport to show all the intricacies of flaking techniques, but merely the various general shapes or styles of projectile points. In many cases, professional assistance may be needed to classify a point and even then, all authorities may not be in agreement.

**Paleo Projectile Points
20,000 B.C. - 6,000 B.C.**

**Archaic Projectile Points
6,000 B.C. - 1,000 A.D.**

**Woodland Projectile Points
1,000 A.D. - 1,700 A.D.**

Sandia I
Point
(Paleo)

Sandia II
Point
(Paleo)

Sandia III
Point
(Paleo)

Clovis
Point
(Paleo)

Ross County
Point
(Paleo)

Redstone
Point
(Paleo)

Cochise
Point
(Paleo)

Midland
Point
(Paleo)

Folsom
Point
(Paleo)

Beaver Lake
Point
(Paleo)

Holcombe
Point
(Paleo)

Debert
Point
(Paleo)

Plainview
Point
(Paleo)

Dalton Colbert
Point
(Paleo)

Dalton Greenbrier
Point
(Paleo)

Cumberland
Point
(Paleo)

Browns Valley
Point
(Paleo)

Hi-Lo
Point
(Paleo)

Hardaway
Point
(Paleo)

Gypsum Cave
Point
(Paleo)

Quad
Point
(Paleo)

Pelican
Point
(Paleo)

Wheeler Triangular
Point
(Paleo)

Wheeler Recurvate
Point
(Paleo)

Breckenridge
Point
(Paleo)

Agate Basin
Point
(Paleo)

Hell Gap
Point
(Paleo)

Milnesand
Point
(Paleo)

Lake Mohave
Point
(Paleo)

Angostura
Point
(Paleo)

Alberta
Point
(Paleo)

Scottsbluff I
Point
(Paleo)

Scottsbluff II
Point
(Paleo)

Eden
Point
(Paleo)

Greenbrier
Point
(Paleo)

Meserve
Point
(Paleo)

Allen
Point
(Paleo)

Golondrina
Point
(Paleo)

Nebo Hill
Point
(Paleo)

Sedalia
Point
(Paleo)

Rio Grande
Point
(Paleo)

Pinto Basin
Point
(Paleo)

Silver Lake
Point
(Paleo)

Abilene
Point
(Paleo)

Short-Stemmed
Point
(Archaic)

Long-Stemmed
Point
(Archaic)

Eared
Point
(Archaic)

Tapered-Stem
Point
(Archaic)

Side-Notched
Point
(Archaic)

Long-Eared
Point
(Archaic)

Small-Stemmed
Point
(Archaic)

Corner-Notched
Point
(Archaic)

Triangular
Bottom-Notched
Point
(Archaic)

Triangular
Point
(Archaic)

Leaf-Shaped
Point
(Archaic)

Stemmed
Point
(Archaic)

McKean
Point
(Archaic)

Duncan
Point
(Archaic)

Hanna
Point
(Archaic)

Green River
Point
(Archaic)

Glendo
Point
(Archaic)

Glendo
Point
(Woodland)

Reed
Point
(Woodland)

Washita
Point
(Woodland)

Harrell
Point
(Woodland)

Leaf-Shaped
Point
(Woodland)

Triangular
Point
(Woodland)

Bottom-Notched
Point
(Woodland)

Corner-Notched
Point
(Woodland)

Stemmed
Point
(Woodland)

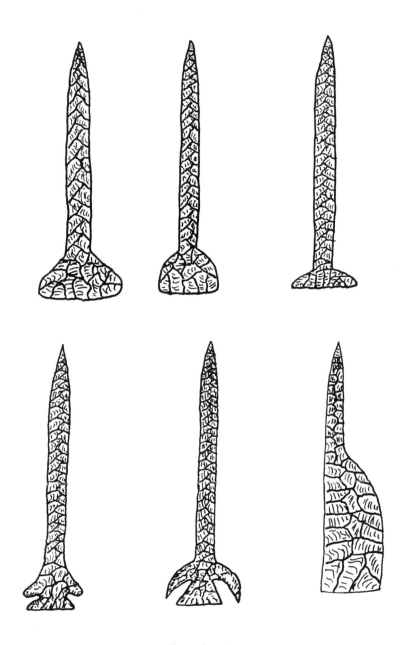

Illustration 33

Assorted "T"-shaped drills and similar drills that should be compared with the typical awls in illustration number 34.

CHAPTER 4

Stone Artifacts

Perforation Artifacts

The Drill

Of all the artifacts other than arrowheads, the drill is one of the more fascinating and delicate implements which the Indian made. There is some problem here in common terminology. Various archaeologists and authorities use the term "awl" interchangeably or in place of the term "drill." The artifact that I am about to describe I prefer to call a drill. I will afterwards describe and illustrate what I consider to be an awl.

The true drill is a finely worked and delicate oblong tool that was ordinarily "T" shaped. The drill must have broken rather easily with use, for in hunting artifacts for over thirty years, I have yet to find a perfect one. I have several bases, tips, and center sections, but not a single complete drill. It is my speculation that most of the perfect drills were either found many years ago or are found through excavation.

The drill was used primarily for drilling holes in leather or hides. The hides would then be sewn together to make clothing. Animal sinew was used as thread. Drills were also used to make holes in bone, rock, mineral, and wood used in the manufacture of implements, beads, and other items.

I have seen tips of drills that were as sharp as a pin and others that were well worn. Resharpening must have been a necessity with continued use of this artifact, unless the drill broke completely, in which event it was probably discarded. Some archaeologists believe that broken drills were many times refashioned into arrowheads.

Drills have also been known to be made of bone and antler. Most of these types of drills are found through supervised excavation of sites below the surface where they have been preserved by nature. A bone or antler drill is next to impossible to find on the surface due to rapid deterioration that is helped on by the action of mice and other rodents who find the material to be a good source of calcium. The illustrations shown herein depict drills made of flint or other flint-type materials. You will notice that the drill was made for use either by holding in the hand or for hafting to a shaft. Illustration number 33 shows some of the types of "T"-shaped drills that can be found.

The Awl

The awl, as opposed to the drill, is not ordinarily found as much in the common "T" shape of a nail as is the drill, and many times may be nearly as wide as it is long. The awl was almost always held in the hand rather than notched and hafted to a shaft. The awl, like the drill, was principally used to make a hole in another material such as a hide. Also, the artifact that I consider to be an awl was ordinarily made only of flint or flint-type materials. Sometimes the awl is bifacial, or worked on both sides, but many times it is unifacial, or worked only on one side. Frequently the awl is domed and is not always as thin as a drill or a finely worked arrowhead. The perfect awl seems to be more common than the perfect drill, primarily because the drill broke easier during usage and while lying on the ground than did the awl. An awl is often found in perfect condition other than perhaps a worn or slightly broken tip. More often than not, the awl is made with a natural indentation for the thumb or forefinger to aid in using the tool. On close examination, the awl may fit perfectly into either the right or left hand. Following are illustrations of some of the awls that I have found in northern Colorado and southern Wyoming. (See illustration number 34.) Illustration number 35 shows awls that are two to three inches long and one to two inches wide at the widest point.

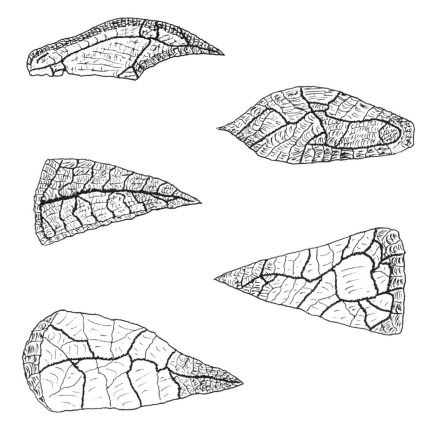

Illustration 34

Various types of awls illustrated by the author from his own collection found by his family.

Illustration 35
Awls found by the author and his family.

The Graver

The graver is an interesting stone artifact that is difficult to find, at least in areas where I have hunted, but that might be common in other parts of the country. A graver is also one artifact that could be overlooked easily as just another piece of flint. It is not easily recognized in the field and must be actually picked up and closely inspected for the presence of a very small amount of workmanship. The graver is basically a small flake of flint or flint-type material usually containing one small spur on one edge. Sometimes the flake will contain more than one spur, but this type is extremely rare. The spur will generally be small and short and sometimes may reveal a very minimal amount of workmanship. Very close inspection and sometimes a good deal of speculation are required to identify gravers. Others may on occasion be easily recognized.

The graver was used to perforate or penetrate thin hides and leather much in the same manner as the awl or drill, but it was obviously not fitted for the heavier use of the awl or drill. Some

  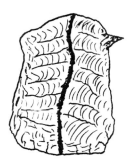

Illustration 36
Three typical types of gravers.

archaeologists maintain that the graver was used primarily for etching or artwork by the Indian and perhaps even for tatooing of the skin. These possible uses certainly cannot be overlooked. The graver is an interesting and somewhat mysterious artifact, to say the least. The gravers shown in illustration number 36 are approximately the size of a silver dollar.

Scraping and Cutting Artifacts

The Scraper

Almost any good-sized piece of flint or flintlike material could have been used as a scraper in one way or another, and a good imagination may come in handy in trying to identify one. Scrapers are found frequently, perhaps more so than arrowheads or any other artifact for that matter. Sometimes, however, the finely worked, perfect scraper is as hard to find as the perfect arrowhead.

Scrapers range in size from those as small as a thumbnail (from which the thumb scraper takes its name), to those as large as the palm of the hand. They were used primarily in scraping hides, bones, and other similar materials in the preparation of food, clothing, and shelter. The true scrapers, as distinguished from those that require a certain degree of speculation or imagination, are generally not hard to identify. The workmanship and shaping of the flint material, for example, is often delicate and deliberate, and at least one good scraping edge of the artifact is easily recognizable by even an inexperienced person. Generally, the scraper is worked or shaped on one side only, with the reverse side being smooth, unworked, and many times concave in shape, caused primarily by the manner in which the flint material originally fractured. The bifacial scraper, or one that has been worked on both sides, is somewhat thicker than the stone knife, which is very similar in appearance but usually quite thin when compared to a scraper. To further complicate identification, a scraper could many times be used as a knife, for these implements were often interchangeable. I once helped skin an antelope with an artifact that I first considered to be a scraper. This artifact also worked well in scraping the antelope hide after completion of the skinning process. I have since categorized the artifact as a knife, mainly because it is thin and worked on both sides.

Many times the thumb scraper in particular will have a perfect indentation for thumb placement. Also, the worked side of the scraper often has a visible "ridge" running almost the full length of the artifact which resulted from the original fracture of the flint in the flaking process.

Scrapers are generally categorized as thumb or thumbnail scrapers; side scrapers; end scrapers; side and end scrapers; and snub-nosed scrapers, which categorization usually depends upon the location of the worked edge on the artifact. The side and end scrapers are shown in illustration number 37. The top and side views shown at the bottom of the illustration reveal the slight ridge running almost the full length of the artifact on top, caused by the original fracture of the material. In the side view, you can also see the turtle-back or hump-back characteristic of the artifact. The smaller thumb scrapers and snub-nose scrapers shown in illustration number 38 have the same general characteristics as the larger scrapers in illustration number 37. Most of these scrapers are no larger than a quarter or a fifty-cent piece. Illustration numbers 39 and 40 show the same scrapers from both the top and the bottom or underside view.

To find scrapers, you have to be able to recognize the smooth, concave feature of the underside of the scraper showing no workmanship of the flint at all. It may be passed over very easily

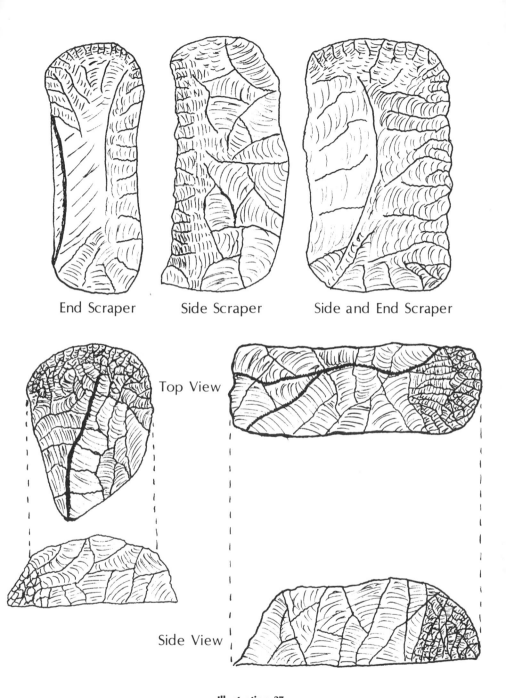

End Scraper   Side Scraper   Side and End Scraper

Top View

Side View

Illustration 37
Various types of larger scrapers illustrated in actual size from the author's family collection.

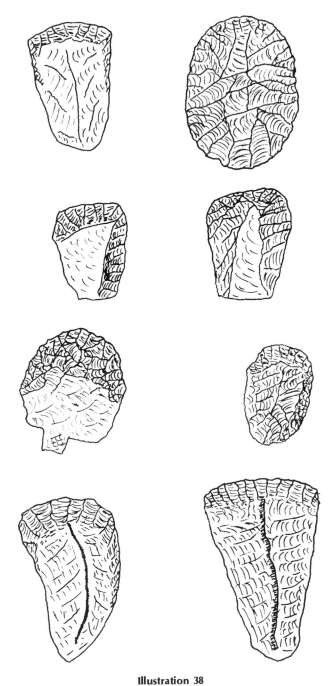

Illustration 38

Various types of smaller thumb scrapers illustrated in actual size from the author's family collection.

Illustration 39

Assorted unifacial scrapers shown in this photograph from what could be considered the top, or worked side, of the scraper. Illustration number 40 shows the same scrapers from the bottom, or unworked side, of the scraper.

as just another flake of flint unless you actually turn it over after recognizing it as a possible scraper. I have turned over many nice scrapers with my hunting stick without ever bending over. It is always a pleasant surprise to find the beautiful workmanship on the reverse side of the scraper after turning it over. Sometimes the pieces have to be picked up and examined very closely to see the delicate chipping workmanship along the edge. It would be easy to discard a scraper like this after a careless and quick examination. Always remember that rarely is there any reason to be in a hurry. Take time to study the artifact closely in the field, or at least take it home and study it further under a good light.

Many artifact collectors do not have much regard for the scraper, perhaps because scrapers are relatively common and not

Illustration 40

Bottom or unworked side of scrapers shown in illustration number 39. Note the characteristic flat or concave smoothness on this side resulting from the natural flaking process of the flint material.

as fascinating as the arrowhead. Archaeologists, however, find the scraper to be just as interesting and valuable in their studies as the arrowhead itself. I have always maintained that I would rather find a nice scraper than a broken arrowhead. The delicate workmanship on many scrapers is indeed a fascinating work of art.

The Knife

The flint knife is somewhat similar to the scraper, although it is generally longer, thinner, and larger than the scraper and normally is bifacial rather than unifacial. Sometimes, in fact, the flint knife will have a striking resemblance to a typical steel hunting knife, although generaly it is not as long. The knife was obviously used to cut various materials such as meat, hides, wood, and fibrous food products.

Many knives that I have found are sharp enough to get the job done! With flint comparing in degree of hardness to steel, it is easy to see that this was an invaluable tool.

Most knives are simply categorized as knives, with no particular subcategories, as with scrapers. Some, however, will have only one cutting edge, while others will have two to four cutting edges, such as the knives shown in illustration number 41. Generally, the smaller the knife, the more cutting edges it will

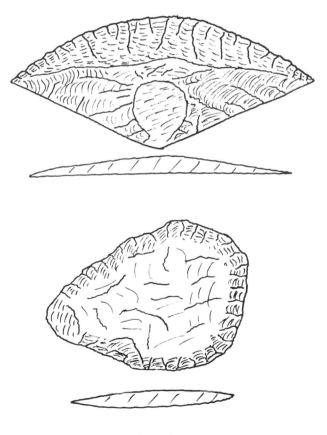

Illustration 41

Various types of knives illustrated in actual size from the author's family collection.

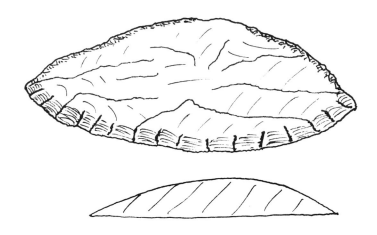

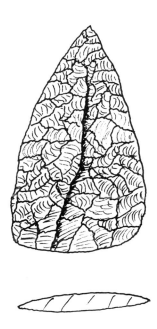

Illustration 41 (continued)
Various types of knives illustrated in actual size from the author's family collection.

Illustration 42
The larger single-edge knives from the author's family collection shown in the top row, as compared with the smaller multi-edge, leaf-shaped knives on the bottom row.

Cody Knife   Tang Knife

Illustration 43
The classical Cody and Tang knives.

have, and the larger the knife, the fewer cutting edges it will have. (See illustration number 42.) Two knives that come to mind that have been categorized are the Tang knife and the Cody knife, shown in illustration number 43. I have never found one of these fascinating knives because they are rare. The Tang knife was no doubt made for hafting onto a wooden shaft—note the characteristic notches on the Tang knife. The remaining large knives pictured in illustration number 44 have more than one cutting edge and may, in fact, have also been used as scrapers. These are the kinds of artifacts that are very difficult to categorize without a certain amount of speculation.

Illustration 44

The larger bifacial leaf-shaped knives, which could have also been used as scrapers.

The Blade

The blade is an oblong piece or flake of flint material that was generally not worked but that could serve as a knife without really having a cutting edge worked on it. It normally resulted from a natural fracturing of the flint material from the larger

Illustration 45
The macroblade at the top compared with the microblade on the bottom shown
somewhat larger than the actual artifacts.

mother core. The larger blade has been referred to as the
macroblade, while the smaller blade has been called a
microblade. Occasionally, these blades will show evidence of
unifacial or bifacial working along one edge and will often have a
ridge running the full length of the blade. This ridge has caused
some authorities to refer to these blades as "prismatic" flakes
because of their prismlike appearance. The true prismatic flake
or microblade is rarely found in the areas with which I am
familiar, although they are perhaps more common in other parts
of the country. (See illustration number 45.) The microblade
shown at the bottom of the illustration is actually only one-half
inch wide and one and one-half inches long.

The Chisel or Gouge

The chisel could also be easily mistaken for a knife or scraper. Its use, however, was probably not for scraping or cutting, as with a knife, but rather for gouging or chipping, as with the modern cold chisel used in woodworking. In fact, with a bit of imagination, it does resemble the modern cold chisel, although it is usually somewhat shorter in length. (See illustration number 46.)

Illustration 46
The chisel.

The Chopper or Slitter

The chopper is, likewise, an artifact that could easily be mistaken for a knife or scraper unless it is notched for attachment to a shaft. It has sometimes been referred to as a "slitter." The use of a chopper or slitter is practically the same as for a knife. This artifact is ordinarily almond shaped, as are many knives. When notched and worked on only one edge, it gives the appearance of half of an arrowhead. (See illustration number 47.)

Illustration 47
A stemmed chopper or slitter shown on the left, compared with the single, corner-notched chopper or slitter illustrated on the right.

The Saw

The flint saw is also similar to the knife, but it is distinguishable primarily because its cutting edge is much more coarse or serrated than the finely worked knife edge. In effect, it does resemble the typical handheld modern rip saw blade. The only stone saw that I have found is approximately four to five inches long with one roughly serrated cutting edge. It was definitely sharp enough to cut most any material. (See illustration number 48.)

Illustration 48
The saw.

The Crescent

The crescent is a very fascinating and rare stone artifact in the cutting category. Some archaeologists believe that the crescent is found only in and about sites containing the prehistoric Paleo points. This may well be true, because the only one I have found was in an area where I had previously found a classical Folsom point in eastern Colorado. Interestingly enough, the flint material was exactly the same material as the Folsom point. Furthermore, some archaeologists have speculated that perhaps the crescent originally came from the flute that was struck from the face of the Folsom point and that gave the Folsom point its unique appearance. This theory definitely has merit.

The crescent can be either concave or convex and many times is also quarter-moon in appearance, with one sharply worked cutting edge drawing to a point on one end. The crescent is usually made of good quality flint-type material such as jasper or chalcedony. (See illustration number 49.) A somewhat larger crescent, perhaps five or six inches long, has been found in California to a limited extent and has been termed the Stockton curve. As far as I know, this particular form of the crescent is extremely rare.

Illustration 49
The crescent.

The All-Purpose Tool

The all-purpose tool is a rare stone artifact that would logically fit into the perforating, cutting, and scraping categories. Its use as a grinding artifact is unlikely. This artifact is normally larger than a thumb scraper or a drill but smaller than a large knife or scraper. The all-purpose tool always has one end worked to a point for perforation, with the opposite end worked in the form of an end scraper. One side is worked rather delicately for use as a knife. It is almost always oblong in shape and generally fits either the right or left hand quite well. Illustration number 50 shows the versatility of this stone artifact. This artifact can be difficult to distinguish from the awl, as the two are similar in shape.

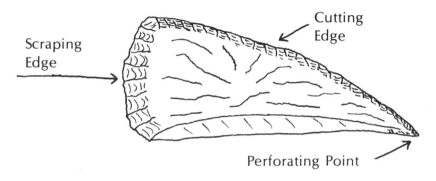

Scraping Edge

Cutting Edge

Perforating Point

Worked Point

Worked Cutting Edge

Worked Scraping Edge

End View

Illustration 50

Illustration of the basic construction and uses of the all-purpose tool shown in actual size from the author's family collection.

The Adze

Another cutting artifact very similar to and hard to distinguish from the chisel is known as the adze. The adze was perhaps generally longer and wider than the chisel and was many times shaped like an axe blade. The adze was made from hematite and from the flint materials by both percussion and pressure-flaking techniques. It was, like the chisel, used in woodworking and can vary anywhere from one and one-half to eight inches in length. The adze normally has one flat side, with the opposite side somewhat convex in nature. (See illustration number 51.)

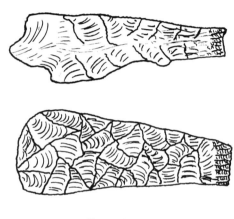

Illustration 51
The adze.

The Burin

The burin is a stone tool that may be classified as a cutting implement similar to the chisel, adze, and graver. Like the graver, it was used primarily as a scoring or engraving tool, and yet, in appearance, it more closely resembles the chisel or adze. It was probably smaller than the adze and hard to differentiate from a small chisel. Generally, one end (the incising end) will be finely worked by pressure flaking. (See illustration number 52.) Illustration number 53 shows a comparison of what I believe to be a narrow knife, a wide drill, and an adze or burin, in that order from left to right. Note the similarity in appearance of the artifacts.

Illustration 52
The burin.

Illustration 53
These three artifacts included for comparison are categorized by the author as a knife, drill, and adze, from left to right.

The Axe

The stone axe is an interesting forerunner of the modern-day axe used primarily for chopping wood. Very few of these artifacts are made of the flint materials, and most of them were shaped by pecking and grinding of igneous rock such as granite, hematite, iron ore, and occasionally sandstone or limestone. Normally the stone axe is one of the larger stone artifacts. It can range from one to twenty pounds in weight. This artifact is usually grooved for hafting onto a wooden handle. The grooved axe shown in illustration number 54 is actually better depicted in illustration number 55. It may be distinguished from the maul or hammerstone by the groove and sharp edge, as compared to the rounded or blunt end of the maul or hammerstone. The hand axes shown in illustration number 56 are basically the same artifact without the grooved feature.

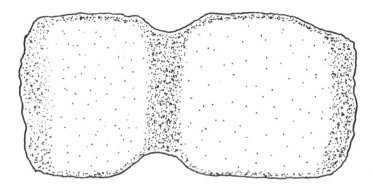

Illustration 54
The typical stone axe illustrated.

Illustration 55
Two common, although hard to find, grooved axes.

Illustration 56
Two typical hand axes.

Scalping Knife

The scalping knife is a stone artifact that can easily be mistaken for a curved awl or drill. Perhaps the awl or drill, if curved, would be smaller and more delicately worked. The scalping knife is most usually made from the flint materials and is long, thin, curved, and very sharp edged. Some were handheld for use and others were hafted onto a bone or wood handle. My experience leads me to the conclusion that this artifact is also extremely rare. (See illustration number 57.)

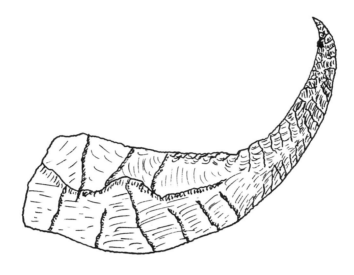

Illustration 57
Scalping knife.

Spokeshaves

The spokeshave is an interesting and somewhat rare stone artifact. It is usually made from the flint materials and can be easily mistaken for a scraper or knife. Normally the spokeshave is smaller than a knife and can be distinguished by having one or more indentations on the sides. It is speculated that this stone

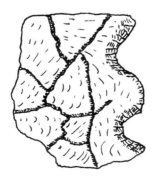 

Illustration 58
Spokeshaves.

artifact was used to shave or scrape down the wooden arrows in order to get a more perfectly rounded arrow for better flight. Much of the wood used for arrows was not perfectly round because of small twigs and bends. The spokeshave was used much like the old draw knife was used in removing bark from a log. The spokeshave is shown in illustration number 58.

Grinding and Pounding Artifacts

Mano and Metate

The mano and metate are generally described hand in hand, since they were normally used together in grinding. The mano, otherwise known as a milling or grinding stone, could have conceivably been used alone in grinding, but the metate could

Oval-Shaped River Rock

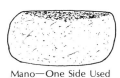

Mano—One Side Used

Mano—Two Sides Used

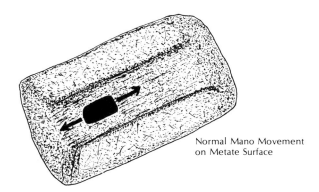

Normal Mano Movement
on Metate Surface

Illustration 59

Variations of the mano, or grinding stone, showing degrees of wear from the original smooth river rock to flattening of both sides. At the bottom, the normal use of the mano on the metate, or grinding slab, is illustrated.

only be used together with the mano. The metate, or grinding slab as it is commonly known, was just as its name implies—a stone slab used as a grinding platform. The handheld mano or grinding stone was moved back and forth or in a circular fashion on the surface of the slab to grind food from a coarse substance into a finer substance. (See the bottom of illustration number 59.) Illustration number 60 shows a mano on a metate that is not grooved or worn down by mano movement back and forth, but rather in an uneven or circular manner.

Illustration 60
Mano and metate.

The grinding stone was hardly ever made from flint material, probably because of the hardness of flint and the sharp edges left on flint as a result of the conchoidal fracturing. A far more suitable stone for grinding was a smooth, well-worn river rock, generally granite or similar material. The smooth river rock was more comfortable to the palm of the hand and could probably have been used for several hours with little discomfort.

Most grinding stones are four to six inches in length, three to four inches in width, and two to three inches in thickness— usually somewhat larger than a clenched fist and oblong or round in shape. Generally both sides of the stone have been flattened through heavy usage upon the grinding slab, although many times a stone will only have one side flattened. Many grinding stones when flattened on both sides will resemble a new bar of soap. Illustration number 59 also shows, at the top, the various forms of manos that can be found according to wearing patterns.

The grinding stone is a common find in the northern Colorado foothills and the plains of eastern Colorado, primarily because these areas were more suitable for farming than the higher mountain elevations. Corn, for example, could only be grown in the lower elevations and was probably ground extensively with the mano and metate. On the other hand, the grinding stone can be found in the higher mountain elevations where berries grew wild and were ground by the Indian in food preparation.

Over the years, I have found several grinding stones on open and steep ridge areas above campsites. This has led me to conclude that they were also used to prepare hides for clothing and shelter. Many that I have found were in close association with scrapers of all sizes and types in areas above campsites. Although it is possible that food could have been ground in the high areas above campsites, it seems more logical that hides would have been scraped, smoothed, and prepared for clothing and shelter in open areas away from the campsite itself.

Although the grinding stone is commonly found, it is not always easy to find. Many times it may appear on the surface as just another rock until it is turned over to reveal the flattened grinding surface. Any smooth or round river rock should at least be turned over and examined, especially in an area that is a good distance from the nearest creek or river. It may be "foreign" to the area and may well be a grinding stone left by man rather than by nature. Illustration number 61 shows the natural top side of a grinding stone, once probably a river rock. It does not appear to be an artifact at all. Illustration number 62, however, shows the bottom side of the same stone flattened and worn down considerably through use as a grinding stone. Again, any foreign rock of this type, especially in a known campsite, should be

Illustration 61

This photograph shows the top, or smooth, natural side of the river rock. Compare with the next photograph in illustration number 62, which shows the bottom, or worn side, of the same river rock.

Illustration 62

Worn side or bottom of river rock shown in illustration number 61.

turned over and inspected.

The metate, or grinding slab, on the other hand, is very rare and difficult to find on the surface. My theory is that the grinding slab was usually large—really one of the largest stone artifacts that can be found—and because of this, the majority of the surface artifacts were probably found many years ago. Also, there still may be several that were turned over in the campsites and that now appear as ordinary rock slabs. I believe that when Indians temporarily left a campsite, they would simply turn the metates over so that the implements would not collect rainwater and snowmelt and then freeze and break. Upon return to the campsite, the Indians could then turn over the metates and use them again. They were generally too heavy for transportation, often weighing from twenty-five to seventy-five pounds. Farmers on the Colorado plains will occasionally plow up a metate in a field, but most seem to be found during archaeological excavation.

Illustration 63
Various assortment of manos.

The metate generally is twelve to eighteen inches in width, eighteen to twenty-four inches in length, and two to four inches thick, and, of course, is flat in overall appearance. The majority of the time the metate will have a hollowed out or depressed appearance usually on one surface only, caused by the grinding and sliding movement of the mano back and forth. The metate will likewise not ordinarily be made of flint material, but rather from granite or sometimes a sandstone or sandstonelike material. Certain volcanic materials were also used for both metates and manos.

Many times at a campsite, several broken manos and perhaps a broken metate may be found with an obvious lack of a whole mano or metate. One of two theories may explain this situation. First, if Indians abandoned a campsite, they would probably leave behind any broken tools, especially the heavier ones. Second, some authorities feel that any time Indians abandoned a campsite, they would intentionally break their manos and metates perhaps as a ritual. Illustration number 63 shows an assortment of various manos or grinding stones that I have found over the years. Note how similar they are.

Hammerstone or Percussor

The hammerstone or percussor is similar to the grinding stone in appearance, size, and material used. Many times igneous river rocks were also used as hammerstones, probably because of their smooth surface that would have been more comfortable to the hand. The hammerstone, as compared with the maul, was used in the hand only and was not grooved for hafting onto a wood handle, as was the maul. Other than this, the artifacts are very similar in usage and appearance. Sometimes, in fact, a mano was also used as a hammerstone, in which event, the ends of the stone, rather than being rounded, will have a broken or chipped appearance. The hammerstone was generally used in breaking larger "mother" cores of flint material into smaller flakes and spalls to be used for arrowheads, scrapers, and the like. This was normally accomplished by either direct percussion (one stone against the other) or by indirect percussion, such as an antler being held in the hand as an intermediate tool between the hammerstone and the larger flint material. See the hammerstone or percussor in illustration number 64.

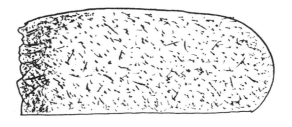

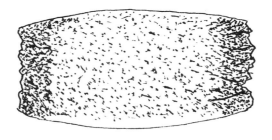

Illustration 64
The hammerstone or percussor.

Mortar and Pestle

Another set of grinding artifacts that seem to be rare in northern Colorado and southern Wyoming are the mortar and pestle. They may be more common in other parts of the country, such as the Southwest. This is understandable, since much Indian art comes out of the Southwest, and the mortar and pestle were commonly used to grind substances for painting pottery. In this respect, pottery sherds are also relatively rare in northern Colorado and southern Wyoming. This may be because pottery was not made or used as much in the higher elevations as it was in the Southwest or lower elevations. Furthermore, pottery not being truly a stone artifact, deteriorates much more readily in the harsher climates and simply is not commonly found except for very small pieces. It is also easy to speculate that the mortar and pestle were used in grinding food substances, such as small amounts of salt. With the mano and metate commonly used, however, it is difficult to imagine why the Indian would have

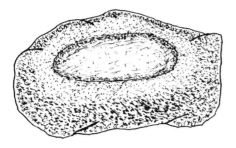

Illustration 65

Mortar and pestle.

Illustration 65a

Stone mortar.

used the mortar and pestle in grinding food substances other than, perhaps, various medicinal herbs.

The mortar and pestle were generally made from sandstone, granite, or similar materials and were not ordinarily made from the flint materials. The mortar was usually about the size of a small bowl and, in fact, looks much like a small cereal bowl. The depression area in the center will be hollowed out and smooth from the circular grinding of the pestle. The pestle is oblong and may be somewhat larger on the grinding end as compared with the handheld end. The pestle is also made from sandstone or granite or other similar materials. The mortar and pestle are shown in illustration number 65. A very unique stone mortar found in western Nebraska is shown in illustration number 65a.

Shaft Straightener or Abrader

Another interesting stone artifact is the abrader, which I prefer to call a shaft straightener. This implement was ordinarily used to straighten arrows upon which the arrowhead was attached on one end. The arrows themselves were usually made from branches of the wild cherry, birch, ash, or willow trees when these trees were available, because their wood was harder and more durable. Many times, of course, the branches were not perfectly straight and contained a number of knots where smaller twigs and branches had been removed. The shaft straightener was used by the Indian to grind or smooth out the arrow shaft and correct these imperfections. The artifact itself was normally made of sandstone when available. Other rock was used on occasion, but generally not any of the flint materials. Most shaft straighteners are somewhat small—perhaps two to four inches wide, six to eight inches long, and one to two inches thick. They will always have at least one and sometimes two grooves running lengthwise or crosswise on one surface. These grooves, of course, are formed by sliding the shaft back and forth across the surface. They become deeper with increased usage. Initially, the grooves may have been made by using bone, antler, or rock. As strange as it may seem, these artifacts are not common, at least in my part of the country. I have only one artifact that may have been used as a shaft straightener, and it is questionable when compared to the true specimens shown in illustration number 66.

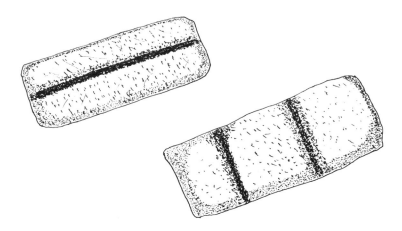

Illustration 66
Abrader or shaft straightener.

Illustration 67
The maul or hammer.

Maul or Hammer

The stone maul can be thought of as the forerunner of the modern sledge hammer, for it is very similar in appearance. It can be distinguished from the hammerstone in that the hammerstone was typically held in the hand and used without a handle. The maul was grooved for hafting, just as the axe was used with a wooden handle. It can be distinguished from the axe by its rounded or blunt end as compared with the sharper edge of the stone axe. Similarly, the maul was also made by pecking and grinding of igneous rock, as flint material was rarely used. The maul can also weigh anywhere from one to twenty pounds. (See illustration number 67.)

Miscellaneous Utility Artifacts

Hoe

The stone hoe may be thought of as the forerunner of the modern garden hoe, as it was used primarily in farming or

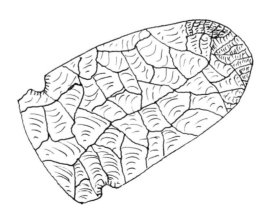

Illustration 68
The hoe.

gardening by the Indian. For this reason, it is rarely found in the higher mountain campsites where agriculture was not generally practiced. The hoe is normally an isolated find in lowland and prairie campsites where agriculture *was* generally practiced. It is usually a well-chipped artifact made of the flint materials, generally thinner than the axe and maul and approximately five inches wide and ten inches long. It was notched or grooved for hafting onto a wooden handle or was sometimes hafted without the aid of notches or grooves. Many are smooth or shiny due to heavy usage in the soil. (See illustration number 68.)

Stone Balls

Round stone balls of all sizes are not an uncommon find in and about ancient Indian campsites. Many theories have been expounded as to the exact use of these artifacts, and some people may frown at any speculation that they are even artifacts. They are common, however, in campsites and, in my opinion, enough evidence exists of their usage that their presence is more than coincidental. They do not seem to be a popular artifact in collections, probably because they all essentially look alike, except sometimes for size.

Most stone balls are made by pecking and polishing, rather than chipping of flint materials. Igneous rock and sandstone were generally used in making the stone ball. Stone balls can generally be classified as game stones, cooking stones, hot stones, and ceremonial stones.

There is not much evidence of their use as game or ceremonial stones, although it is easy to speculate that they may have been used by children in playing games or, because of their shape, used in ceremonial rituals. Good evidence exists, however, for their use as cooking stones and hot stones. This evidence is primarily the fire-reddened color of many of these stone balls. When a rock is heated for a long time, or several times, it will develop this fire-reddened appearance. Stone balls may have been heated as cooking stones and placed in water or perhaps in stews in order to convey heat and thereby heat the water or stew. Also, stone balls may have been laid on top of red hot coals, and then meat laid on top of the stone balls to cook. Where stone balls are found in areas containing black rock and ash or charcoal, and especially in an area where an Indian would have built a fire, good evidence exists that the stone ball was used in cooking. In fact, the ones I have found were fire-reddened and found in exactly this type of an area. Their use in cooking seems unquestionable to me.

It has also been said that stone balls were similarly heated and used as hot stones at hide-working sites. They were placed on the hides while red hot and used to burn or scorch off undesirable materials.

Most of the stone balls that I have found are about the size of a golf ball, although many are both smaller and larger. My theory is that the golf-ball size stones were used in cooking, the smaller ones used games, such as marbles, and the larger ones perhaps used in ceremonies and games. Some have been found as large as bowling balls and may have, in fact, been used as such. Illustration number 69 shows several of these round balls, ranging from the larger ball about the size of a baseball to the smallest ball about the size of a pea.

Illustration 69
Assortment of round stones, from the small, pea-sized stone to the larger baseball-sized stone.

Core

The core, to many collectors, is a very uninteresting artifact, but to the archaeologist, both amateur and professional, it is quite the opposite. The core is the larger "mother flint" from which, through percussion flaking, both direct and indirect, the smaller flakes and spalls were struck and eventually shaped into arrowheads, drills, scrapers, and the like. Core material was actually transported great distances, especially when it consisted of a good quality flint material desirable for making the more delicate artifacts. Most of the cores that I have found were in campsites and high lookout points on ridges where an Indian could have easily made artifacts while on watch duty for the camp. They come in all sizes, shapes, and colors; most that I have found are the size of a baseball or somewhat larger. Illustration number 70 shows the core after a number of smaller flakes and spalls have been struck from the stone, leaving the cuplike conchoidal fractures.

Cuplike Depressions

Conchoidal Fractures

Illustration 70

The core or mother stone from which flakes were struck, leaving the characteristic cuplike depressions of the conchoidal fractures. In actual size, this stone could be as large as a grapefruit or as small as a golf ball.

Fishhook

The stone fishhook normally made of the flint materials is a rare find, especially in areas where little fishing was done. In the northern Colorado mountains where many beaver ponds exist, the Indian could have probably caught more fish by hand rather than going to the trouble of making and using a fishhook. Nevertheless, it is a very interesting and unique stone artifact and one that would be a welcome addition to most any collection. Many stone fishhooks have been found in the coastal regions and in areas of the country that have large rivers and lakes. (See illustration number 71.)

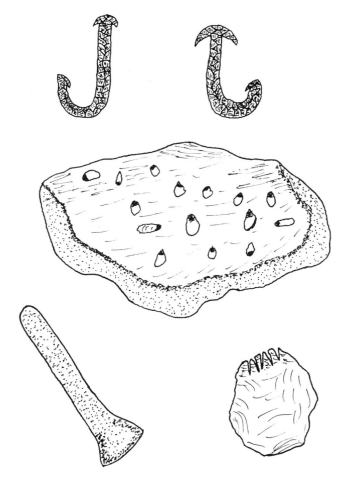

Illustration 71

At the top, two typical flint fishhooks are shown. In the center, the cupstone is illustrated showing the numerous small indentations on top of the larger stone. The spatulate or spud is illustrated at the bottom left, and the sinewstone is shown at the bottom right.

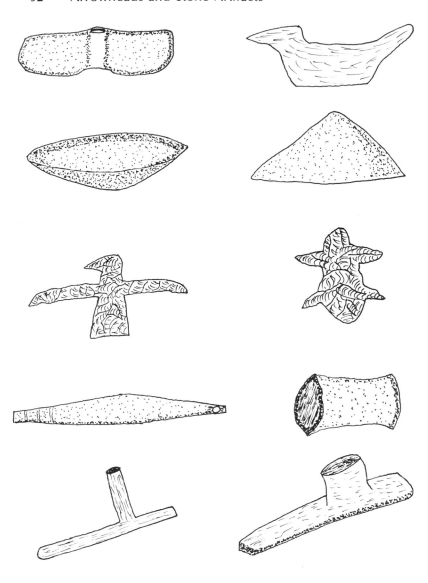

Illustration 72

Assorted ceremonial or ornamental stone artifacts are illustrated as follows:
Top row on left, bannerstone; top row on right, birdstone; second row from top
on left, boatstone; second row from top on right, dome or cone; center row on
the left, bird effigy; center row on the right, turtle effigy; second row from the
bottom on the left, charmstone; second row from the bottom on the right, spool;
bottom row, both right and left, are two examples of stone pipes.

Celt or Tomahawk

The celt, as it is known in the West, is a stone artifact that seems to show up in very few collections, at least in my part of the country. Perhaps it is more common in other areas, or perhaps it is mistaken for a stone axe. It is generally rectangular in shape with a thin, sharp cutting edge. It is usually about two to three inches wide and five to six inches long and is made from the flint materials or occasionally from slate, hematite, or basalt. Furthermore, it is generally not quite an inch thick and can be distinguished from the axe or maul because it is not grooved for hafting onto a wooden handle. It was simply inserted into a slit made in the wooden handle, as shown in illustration number 73. Although it may have been used in warfare, it was more commonly used in fleshing and skinning animal carcasses.

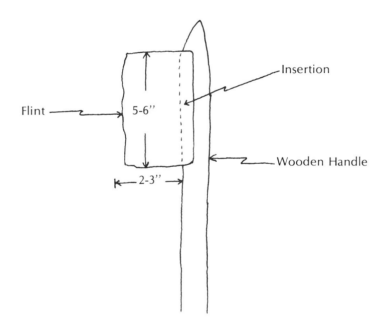

Illustration 73

The celt or tomahawk shown as inserted or hafted onto the wooden shaft or handle.

Moccasin Last

The moccasin last was used to shape leather for moccasins. Although more common in some parts of the country than others, I can recall seeing only one in an artifact collection myself. Generally, the moccasin last was a smooth, igneous-type river rock such as granite. As one might expect, the moccasin last was ordinarily the shape of a footprint. (See illustration number 74.)

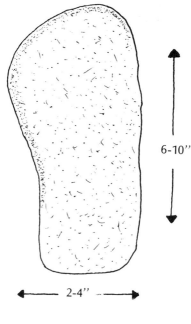

6-10"

2-4"

Illustration 74
The moccasin last.

Rubbing Stone

The rubbing stone is a stone artifact commonly mistaken for the average small river rock, for it is usually very smooth and shiny and generally no larger than the palm of the hand. This artifact could very easily have come from a riverbed initially before being carried to a campsite. It is commonly the same igneous material, such as granite or schist, as the larger river rock used for a grinding stone or mano. It is speculated that the rubbing stone was used in rubbing hides used for clothing and shelter. Its use in grinding herbs and small food materials also cannot be ruled out. It is hard to imagine other possible uses except for perhaps ceremonial purposes. The rubbing stone would probably not be recognized as a stone artifact anywhere but in a campsite location. When one is found in a campsite out of its natural location, it is obvious to me that it was transported to the site for a purpose. I might add that rubbing stones are commonly found in campsites, which is probably not a mere coincidence. A sampling of various rubbing stones can be seen in illustration number 75.

Illustration 75
Assorted rubbing stones.

Whetstone

The whetstone is an unusual stone artifact that is relatively rare, particularly in the Rocky Mountain region with which I am most familiar. It was used to sharpen other artifacts, such as stone or bone drills, simply by rubbing back and forth. These stones are usually less than six inches long and are typically cylindrical in shape so that they fit well in one hand. They usually have a very smooth surface from heavy usage, and only through the visible signs of heavy use can you really determine that a stone is, in fact, a whetstone. Almost any stone material could have been used for a whetstone, and no one material in particular seems to have been used more commonly. A whetstone is shown in illustration number 105 in the bottom left-hand corner.

Cup Stone, Cups, Paint Bowls

These three types of stone artifact have been grouped together because they were, in fact, very similarly used by the Indian. The cup stone has been described by some authorities as being a larger, slablike stone perhaps well over a foot in diameter with several small, cuplike indentations on the surface of one or both sides. These indentations were used as mortars to hold nuts and various other substances which had to be finely ground or broken apart for usage. Normally, a pestle was used to accomplish the breaking or grinding of the substances. I have never personally seen one of these artifacts, and I would suspect that a certain amount of speculation would have to be used to truly identify one.

On the other hand, individual paint bowls or cups have been found that were readily identifiable as stone artifacts. Any naturally hollowed-out stone material could have been used for a bowl or cup, and some appear to have been hollowed out by pecking or grinding. A cup or bowl can be truly identified as a stone artifact if it is discolored by the various substances for which it was used. Certain herbs, berries, or minerals very clearly left permanent, stained discoloration in bowls or cups. For example, minerals, vegetation, and berries were mixed with animal fat to make the various paints used by the Indians. These substances, when mixed and finely ground over and over in the same container, will leave a permanent discoloration clearly different from the natural stone color. In this regard, the minerals iron oxide ore and red ochre were used, leaving a red color; copper ore was used, leaving a green color; and charcoal was used, leaving a black coloration. A small bowl is pictured in illustration number 105 in the upper right-hand corner. The cup stone is shown as the large item in the center of illustration number 71.

Spatulates or Spuds

The spatulate or spud has been recognized and categorized by some archaeological authorities as a flared celt. It was ordinarily eight to ten inches long with a smooth, slender handle and was typically flared out at the base or on the cutting edge. My research indicates that it was ordinarily made from the flint materials by percussion, grinding, and polishing. It was used somewhat like a chisel or knife in dressing hides and debarking trees. Some authorities believe that it may also have been used as a ceremonial object, although in my opinion it was probably used as a tool. The spatulate is shown in illustration number 71 on the lower left-hand side.

Sinewstone

The sinewstone seems to be a very rare stone artifact, and I have personally never seen one. It is usually rather small in order to be held in one hand and may have several incised lines or indentations on one edge where sinew material was drawn back and forth to prepare the material for use as bow strings, thread, or string for fastening or hafting other stone artifacts (such as arrowheads) onto a wooden shaft. Probably any stone material could have been used for the sinewstone, although it would seem that a softer material such as sandstone, soapstone, or slate would have been more appropriately used. The sinewstone is shown in illustration number 71 on the lower right-hand side.

Atlatl Weights

In order to adequately explain the atlatl weight as a stone artifact, you should probably go into a thorough discussion of the atlatl as a device used by prehistoric man to propel or throw a spear before the age of the bow and arrow. Simply stated, the atlatl was usually a rather short, wooden-handle-type device in which the spear was placed and then slung or thrown toward the intended object. A stone weight was often used in conjunction with the device to add velocity or impact to the throw and also to make the device more controllable and accurate. This stone weight, or atlatl weight, was typically made by grinding, polishing, and pecking techniques employed on slate, fireclay, soapstone, siltstone, or catlinite. The stones usually contained one or more drilled holes used for fastening. These weights were ordinarily rather small and were often winged, grooved, and barrel shaped. Bannerstones, birdstones, and boatstones explained in the next section as ornamental or ceremonial stone artifacts are thought by many archaeological authorities to have been primarily used as atlatl weights. These are shown toward the top of illustration number 72.

Ceremonial and Ornamental Artifacts

Effigy

The effigy is a very interesting artifact usually made of stone. It is also rare and hard to find. Effigies are normally made of slate, soapstone, pipestone (or catlinite), or the usual flint materials. They are made by pressure flaking in the case of the flint materials, and by grinding and polishing of the other softer stone materials. The classic thunderbird effigy or eagle is perhaps the more common effigy, but stone effigies of other birds, turtles, fish, lizards, snakes, geese, and trees have also been found. The only practical use of such effigies has always been considered to be ceremonial or ornamental. Two examples of effigies are shown in illustration number 72.

Pendant

The pendant is a stone artifact that sometimes was made of a volcanic material such as basalt. In certain locations, it was made from hematite or slate. It was generally ornamental and most often worn as a necklace. The pendant can be almost any size or shape, but is generally not too large and is quite similar to modern-day jewelry. The pendant may have also been used in ceremonials. It can be distinguished from the amulet and gorget, for it generally has only one small hole drilled entirely through the stone, rather than two holes. (See illustration number 76.)

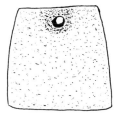

Illustration 76
The pendant.

Gorget

The gorget is another stone artifact that is scarce. I have never found one and can only recall having seen pictures of them or having read about them. The gorget is usually thin and flat, concave on one side and convex on the other, and generally has two holes drilled completely through the stone (usually basalt, hematite, or slate). There are four general theories regarding its use: (1) it was fastened to the left forearm to protect against the slap of the bow string upon shooting an arrow; (2) it was worn ornamentally around the neck; (3) it was used as an object around which to twist twine; and (4) it was used as a shuttle in weaving. The first theory may be the most likely, since several gorgets have been found on left arms in graves. (See illustration number 77.)

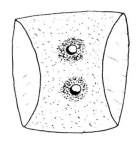

Illustration 77
The gorget.

Amulet

The amulet is yet another comparatively rare stone artifact, at least in my area of the country. I have never found one or ever seen one found. It is usually cigar shaped with a hole perforated through each end. Most amulets are made of slate, hematite, greenstone, or quartz, and some have grooves around the body rather than holes. They may have had the same uses as the gorget. They are, however, generally thicker and longer than the gorget. Also, some think that the amulet may have been the forerunner of the modern string or bolo tie. (See illustration number 78.)

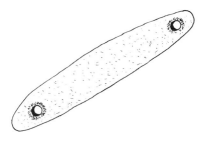

Illustration 78
The amulet.

Discoidal or Disc

The discoidal, commonly called a disc, is a stone artifact that is more common in north-central United States. I have never seen one in a collection in my part of the country, nor have I found one. It is circular in shape and concave on both sides. Quartz or granite was a common material used for this artifact, although some have been found made from standard flint materials, hematite, slate, or basalt. They range from one to nine inches in diameter and from one to twenty pounds in weight. Some have been found with a hole perforated through the center and others simply with flanges around the edges. Many discoidals show very little abuse and seem to have been well cared for. This characteristic leads to the theory that they were used for ritual or ceremonial purposes. Others believe that they were used as small bowls for mixing herbs and seeds to make medicines. (See illustration number 79.)

Illustration 79
The discoidal or disc.

Plummet

The plummet is an interesting stone artifact resembling a carpenter's plumb bob. It is usually made from basalt, slate, or hematite. It is rare; I have never found one nor personally seen one in a collection. The plummet may be several different sizes and shapes but is characteristically marked by a single groove around it toward one end or the middle. Some archaeologists believe that the plummet was used as a sinker for fishing, while others claim that it was a ceremonial or ritual stone of the medicine man, perhaps used in curing the sick or in bringing rain. Still others believe that it was used as a bola stone or worn as a pendant around the neck. The plummet is shown in illustration number 80.

Beads

Most Indian beads were made from shells, bone, pearls, metals, porcupine quills, seeds, teeth, wood, and pottery. Beads were also made from stone, although not exclusively from the flint materials. Any small and pretty stone could be worked into use as a bead, although my research has shown that stone beads are rare when compared to beads of other materials. With the

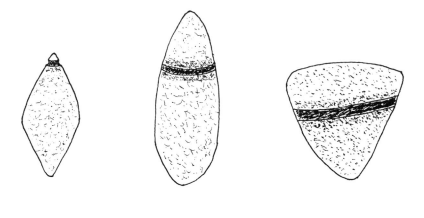

Illustration 80
The plummet.

Illustration 81
Various bead styles.

intrusion of the white man, glass beads were traded for by the Indian and thereby came into common usage. Beads, of course, were primarily ornamental but were also used as wampum, or Indian money, a medium of exchange. Beads can be found in almost any size or shape but are usually circular, cylindrical, or ovular in form, and most always they are perforated for easier stringing. Although beads are widely found throughout the country, I have never had much luck in finding any. Many people claim to have found beads in ant hills probably in the area of a campsite. Some of the general sizes and shapes of beads are shown in illustration number 81.

Stone Pipes

Another interesting and unique stone artifact is the peace pipe or smoking pipe, whose use is surrounded by various legends and theories. While the pipe is not commonly found in the Rocky Mountain area, it is found regularly in other parts of the country, particularly in the Midwest and northern central plains areas. Pipes were made from a number of different materials, including clay, bone, and wood, but perhaps the most unique source material was catlinite, more commonly known as "pipestone."

Pipestone is a unique material found primarily in one area of the United States. Pipestone National Monument has been established by the United States government in a small area of southwestern Minnesota where this material is found in abundance in natural quarries. In fact, some authorities believe that almost all of the catlinite used in making pipes originated in these quarries. It appears to be the only sizeable deposit of catlinite in the entire country. The pipestone itself is specially suited to carving and fashioning into a pipe bowl, and while making a pipe was by no means easy, this material was probably more easily worked than any other material. It would probably be extremely difficult to make a pipe out of flint or one of the related quartzite materials. Catlinite is red in its natural color and is soft when compared to most stone material. In this regard, I would think that pipestone is probably best compared to what is commonly known as "soapstone" or steatite, a soft gray material similar in geological composition. Soapstone is used by the Eskimos and other Indian tribes in making various ornaments and figures, perhaps also including pipe bowls.

Normally only the pipe bowl itself is made out of pipestone, while the pipe stem is usually made from bone or wood. However, some stone pipes are made entirely from pipestone and somewhat resemble an enlarged cigarette holder. In the ordinary manufacturing of the pipestone pipe bowl, a flint knife was used to cut and "rough out" the bowl itself. A wooden shaft with an attached stone drill likely made of flint or a similar quartzite material was used to hollow out the bowl. Scrapers or sandstone were then used to polish and smooth down the rough edges.

While catlinite can be purchased in its natural state and also in the form of various ornaments, including pipe bowls, I am not aware of any location where it can simply be found. It is illegal, of course, to pick it up in Pipestone National Monument. It would appear that outside of the legal purchase of pipestone, the only other way you could obtain a pipestone bowl would be to find a genuine one on an artifact hunting excursion out on the land. While this might be easy in some parts of the country, it would be extremely difficult in the Rocky Mountain area. Two examples of stone pipes are found at the bottom of illustration number 72.

Bannerstone, Birdstone, and Boatstone

These three types of stone artifact have been grouped together because of their similarity, not only in construction but also as either ceremonial or ornamental artifacts or atlatl weights. These implements were typically made from slate, catlinite, or similar soft materials usually by pecking, grinding, and polishing. More often than not, they were drilled with one or more holes perforated entirely through the material. While the birdstone is typically shaped in the form of a sitting or nesting bird and the boatstone is generally a hollowed-out shape like a small boat or canoe, the bannerstone is usually barrel shaped or winged in appearance. Almost all of these artifacts are small and, depending upon the archaeological authority, were used either as ceremonial and ornamental artifacts or, because of their size and construction, were used as atlatl weights. All three artifacts are very rare outside of the Mississippi Valley and north-central United States, including the entire Great Lakes region. The winged, butterfly design bannerstone is one of the most highly treasured artifacts anyone could have in a collection. Three general designs of these artifacts are shown toward the top of illustration number 72.

Cone or Dome, Charmstone, Spool, and Quartz Crystal

The cone or dome is a stone artifact usually made from granite or hematite by pecking and polishing. It is normally small and can be held in one hand. The base is flat with the top pointed or domed—thus the name cone or dome. Its use is speculated to be ceremonial, although not much is really known about the artifact.

Likewise, the charmstone was probably used as a ceremonial piece, with any other use being unlikely. It is generally cylindrical, being somewhat smaller at each end and maybe a few inches in length. Sometimes the charmstone is drilled or perforated. Ordinarily it is made from hematite or granite by pecking and polishing. As with so many of the other ceremonial stone artifacts, it is unusually rare and not found in many artifact collections.

The spool is exactly as the word implies. It is an ordinary spool made from stone, more often sandstone, with a hole perforated lengthwise through the center. Pecking was, no doubt, the sole method of working the stone, and its use was likely ornamental or ceremonial in nature, although an artifact of this type could have easily been used in games. It, too, is extremely rare and not found in many artifact collections. The cone, charmstone, and spool are shown in illustration number 72.

The quartz crystal is a puzzling but rather common find in campsites, and its use seems to have been either ceremonial or ornamental. It is difficult to imagine any other use. Actually, it is hard to categorize the quartz crystal as an artifact at all unless it is found in a known campsite. I have personally found several in campsites and have always suspected that they were used in some fashion by the Indian. My experiences with finding the crystal are not unusual; in fact, some authorities report several instances similar to mine and claim that such quartz crystals were used for ceremonial or ornamental purposes. A quartz crystal that I found in a campsite is shown in illustration number 105, second from the left side in the middle row.

Illustration 82

A typical southeast slope campsite with the actual site shown above the bluffs at the top and down the southeast slope to the right.

CHAPTER 5

WHERE ARTIFACTS ARE FOUND

To find arrowheads and stone artifacts, you obviously have to know where to look for them. You can literally walk for miles and hours and never even find a piece of flint, much less an artifact, unless you have some idea of where you ought to be looking.

A basic understanding of the Indian cultures and habitats of your area is a must in order to "zero in" on productive areas. A good, thorough study of the Indian life-style will give you a better idea of where Indians lived, hunted, and generally spent most of their time. There are, of course, many books available on this subject.

Archaeological sites can be classified into the following categories: (1) habitation or campsites; (2) hunting grounds; (3) blow-out sites; (4) buffalo jump and wallow sites; (5) industrial sites; (6) lookouts; and (7) ceremonial sites.

Campsites

The most common is probably the ordinary campsite, or the place where the Indian lived. Looking for a campsite can be a very interesting and also very frustrating experience. Assuming that you have a basic knowledge of the Indian culture and habitat of your area, some campsites are readily recognizable. The classic campsite, at least in the foothills of Colorado, is the rather high plateau facing or sloping to the east, south, or southeast with a few scattered pine trees and a source of water, such as a stream, spring, or lake, within a quarter of a mile. Quite often a spring is found within the campsite itself feeding a stream or lake lying below to the south or east. This campsite is a typical nonagricultural site. The Indians here depended upon hunting, rather than the growing of crops, for their food supply. This is a permanent campsite, rather than seasonal, especially if found in the lower foothills as opposed to the higher mountains. If this same campsite were found in the high mountains, it would more likely be a seasonal site.

The site will ordinarily be found on a south or east slope, such as the site shown in illustration number 82, because of its relation to the sun in both winter and summer. Also, a south or east slope usually is much more protected from the north and west winds that prevail on the southern Wyoming plains and in the northern Colorado foothills. The main campsite in illustration number 82 is located near the center of the picture on top of the bluffs and down the slope to the right. I have found very few foothill campsites that were directly exposed to a strong northwest wind. The site is usually located on a high point, such as a small plateau or shelf, or on a ridge with an excellent view in at least three and sometimes all four directions. A typical campsite of this kind can be seen in illustration number 83. A campsite located high as opposed to low provided protection from floodwaters and a safe view of intruding enemies, many times from several miles away. A high site was also easier to defend against an enemy and, of course, helped minimize the chances of a surprise attack.

Aside from directional and elevational location, it was essential that a source of water be in the immediate vicinity. In the Colorado foothills, this was ordinarily a spring rather than a lake or stream. The spring usually fed a river or creek somewhere nearby, or at least a natural lake in the general area. In looking for a campsite, be careful to distinguish between the natural and the man-made lake or pond, for it is essential to view an area as it would have existed hundreds of years ago. The dry lakebed site shown in illustration number 84 lies entirely around the dark area in the center of the picture. The dark area was once a natural lake and is clearly indicated by the topography of the area and the darker vegetation and soil in the low area. Even today there is

Illustration 83

A typical bluff or plateau campsite located on the high flat area in the center of the photograph which lies on the south end of the ridge to the right.

Illustration 84

The campsite shown lies entirely around the darker vegetation and dirt area in the center, which is a dry lakebed showing evidence today of subsurface moisture only. The main campsite is located on a south slope above the dry lake.

probably a greater than normal accumulation of subsurface moisture in the former lakebed.

Illustration number 85, on the other hand, shows a typical campsite located on bluffs above a present lake with the creek flowing into it. In this regard, many springs that may have been excellent sources of water several hundred years ago may now be dry and difficult to identify. The same is true with dry creekbeds, although they are usually easier to locate than dry springs due to the terrain. You need to be somewhat familiar with vegetation and its growth in an area once occupied by water. Even though a former spring may now be dry and have no surface water, many times subsurface moisture will still be present and thereby give the area a greener appearance than the surrounding area. A stand of buffalo grass, for instance, may be heavier in a particular area than in the immediate vicinity. Furthermore, many springs even today will dry up in drought years and flow in wet years, so you must constantly observe the

Illustration 85

The campsite shown in this photograph is in the foreground on a small plateau above the lake. The bluffs behind the lake also contain similar small campsite locations.

area for hidden signs. A typical campsite located at a spring is shown in illustration number 86. Of course, there still exist many good, large springs which probably look no different than they did hundreds of years ago. These will be obvious, and many times campsites will be found in the immediate vicinity.

Sometimes ranchers have converted natural springs into small watering ponds, so a campsite might be found by what appears to be a man-made lake as opposed to a natural lake. Here again, you must study the area carefully.

Aside from topographical characteristics, the primary indicator of the campsite is the presence of flint chips either heavily or lightly dispersed through the area. In this regard, you should always check out any ant hills in the area. An ant hill in a campsite will contain thousands of small chips of flint material about the size of a pin head. Ant hills may also contain beads. You must be careful, however, to distinguish between flint material that has been chipped, flaked, or "worked" as opposed

Illustration 86

This campsite at a spring lies entirely around the spring in all directions on both the higher and lower ground.

to a natural outcropping. The campsite will, upon close inspection, have literally hundreds of very small chips present. Many may be no larger than the head of a pin created by the delicate pressure-flaking technique. Others, of course, will be larger, having resulted from percussion flaking. More often than not, the larger cores or "mother flints," some as large as a softball, may be present. Naturally, if the campsite is heavily hunted or perhaps "hunted out," the amount of flint and, indeed, the number of artifacts present, will be reduced considerably. Even then, an area such as this will yield broken arrowheads and scrapers provided the hunter has enough time and patience to look for them.

In any campsite location, you will usually find more bases of arrowheads than tips. You may also find many whole arrowheads that appear to be perfect but that upon close examination will reveal the very fine needle point to be missing. The reason for this appears obvious to me. The Indian, no doubt, came back to camp from hunting with broken arrowheads attached to arrows that had been shot. He probably just detached the bases and broken arrowheads and reattached newly made points to the arrows. Likewise, the broken tips of arrowheads are usually found as stray finds in hunting areas where they were shot and broken off upon impact. Broken tips found in campsites probably resulted from accidental breaking during the original arrowhead-making process. Similarly, many perfect arrowheads can be found in campsite locations perhaps because they were never used in the first place, or the Indian simply left them at a campsite. Every now and then, a completely perfect arrowhead can be found as a stray find in hunting areas. In this event, I think that the arrow was shot and either lost, or simply never retrieved for further use.

Another indicator of a campsite is the presence of the so-called "teepee ring," as shown in illustration numbers 87 and 88. Much discussion and debate have taken place over the "teepee ring" by archaeologists over many years. Some have concluded that teepee rings were used for exactly that purpose; others say that they were ceremonial stone circles and had nothing to do with the teepee. In any event, the presence of circles made from stones is not natural and does indicate the past presence of the Indian one way or another. The rings usually vary from six feet to twenty or thirty feet in diameter. Ordinarily, the stones are underground with only the tops exposed on the surface. This is

Illustration 87

A small teepee ring which I actually drove through on a lightly traveled road before I recognized it as a teepee ring.

Illustration 88

A typical larger teepee ring or perhaps a ceremonial stone circle well disguised by nature.

probably caused by wind or surface water runoff over many years on relatively level ground. The rings are generally found on somewhat level ground as opposed to steeper slopes. Most of the stones themselves are the size of a volleyball or basketball and may be side-by-side or even several feet apart. Some rings are even difficult to distinguish because some of the stones are completely covered up by dirt or perhaps moved out of the original circle by man or animal. I have never found artifacts in or near "teepee rings," although I am told that others have. I have seen several "teepee rings" in the general locality of campsites, however, and I am of the opinion that the rings were more often than not used for ceremonial purposes rather than to hold down the edges of teepees.

My experience in the Colorado foothills has shown me another common and perhaps unusual indicator of a campsite— the presence of yucca plants growing naturally and freely in an area. I have seen a great number of campsites with yucca plants growing in abundance throughout the entire site. A study of early Indian culture reveals that this is not really a coincidence. The Indians used the yucca leaf or fiber as a material for making footwear and other articles of clothing. On occasion, they would weave the fiber together to make utensils and containers such as baskets.

Another indicator of a campsite is the presence of a hearth or pit, which can be difficult to distinguish from the so-called "teepee ring." Generally, the hearth and pit were used for building fires used in cooking and to provide warmth in cold weather. Occasionally, the pit was used for campsite waste materials. The pit was ordinarily deeper in the ground than the hearth, but both the hearth and pit were generally lined with stone. In either case, the soil in the location of a hearth or pit often is discolored—either black soil from charcoal remnants or fire-reddened soil and rocks caused by intense heat. Both the pit and the hearth were usually circular, thereby causing discoloration in the earth in a circular pattern. Therefore, if you encounter a darkened circle of earth, either black or red, it will most certainly be evidence of a campsite. Once again, if any excavation is done, it should be left to the professional archaeologist who can accomplish such a task under proper field conditions.

The presence of pinon trees is another good indicator of a campsite. The early American Indian used the pinon nut as food, and because of this, almost every natural grove of pinon pines will have a campsite located nearby.

On the eastern Colorado and southern Wyoming plains, the campsite ordinarily is found on high knolls and generally not too far from sources of water. A typical knoll site on the plains is shown in illustration number 89. Knolls along creekbeds are usually good areas for campsites in plains areas.

Illustration 89

A typical hilltop or knoll site on the prairie is located on the top of the high area in the center of the photograph.

Hunting Sites

Some archaeological sites on the plains and in the foothills will be found in areas that are *not* located on high ground or near water. These sites may not have been habitation sites, or so-called "campsites," but rather hunting grounds, also sometimes referred to as kill sites. Hunting grounds can be found most anywhere and, of course, many times are on high ground or near springs and other water sources. The main distinguishing feature between the hunting ground and the campsite is the absence of a concentration of many small flint chips. Any pieces of flint material found in hunting grounds are usually pieces of artifacts as opposed to mere chips. The primary determination that must be made is whether or not the flint material has been "worked." To do this, you must look for the characteristic conchoidal fracture that exists as a pattern, rather than by accidental chipping or breaking. Most specimens found in hunting areas will have been worked, while this is not necessarily true in campsites.

Furthermore, some knowledge of game animal habitat will help considerably in discovering hunting areas. Deer, for instance, will travel the higher ridges in the Colorado foothills, while antelope on the plains will many times stay in draws or low-lying areas, probably for protection from high winds. Game animals will also habitually use established game trails in the foothills. Deer, for example, more often than not will cross a ridge in a "saddle" or cut. Also, game animals in the northern Colorado foothills frequently occupy the high east slopes of the many "hogbacks." The high eastern slopes are generally covered with more vegetation than the western sides, which usually drop straight off as cliffs. Many arrowheads can be found as "stray finds" on the hogback hunting grounds. In addition, arrowheads can frequently be found in low-lying hunting grounds along, and actually in, creekbeds, in places generally too low for campsites.

Plowed fields near rivers are always worthwhile for close examination. Generally, it will be difficult to find artifacts in a plowed field until a good rain has washed down the rocks that have been turned to the surface. When first unearthed by the plow, a rock will be covered with dirt and hard to see. Once washed by the rain, the artifact will literally stand out in the surrounding soil.

Blow-Out Sites

In eastern Colorado and many other areas, especially in the West where much sandy native soil still exists, the wind over the years has created areas known as "blow-outs," such as that shown in illustration number 90. Most, but not all, of these blow-outs are on the prairies where the lighter, sandy soil is more common. This type of soil is moved more easily by the wind. Blow-outs can range from a few feet to hundreds of feet in diameter. After a strong wind with little associated moisture, a wide variety of artifacts may be uncovered and easily spotted from several feet away lying alone in the sand. Vegetation in these areas is usually rather sparse, and any foreign material stands out noticeably. Some blow-outs have been created by modern man through plowing. In extremely dry, windy climates, irresponsible soil conservation is not always the cause of these "man-made" blow-outs. Sometimes they simply cannot be helped and probably would have become natural blow-outs in a matter of years anyway. Keep in mind that all natural blow-outs probably started as normal land before the effects of wind erosion took over. Perhaps modern man has simply aided the natural erosion process in some instances.

Illustration 90
A typical blow-out site shown in the entire area of the photograph around the lighter sandy soil.

In any event, blow-outs are typically good places to hunt artifacts wherever they are found. I have never really decided whether the artifacts in blow-outs came from campsites on the location or whether they were generally stray finds. I suspect that in most cases where a large amount of flint or small flint chips are found in the area, the site was probably a campsite at one time, whereas in areas where flint is scarce, the artifacts are probably stray finds resulting from hunting.

Finally, in hunting any blow-out or even a blown area of a field, the better hunting will generally be on the side from which the wind has blown through the area. Usually the ground on this side will be blown clean, exposing many more rocks, while on the opposite side of the blow-out, sand will have accumulated ,perhaps covering up rocks and artifacts. The blow-out has to be closely studied prior to hunting after the most recent windstorm. Wind, of course, can and will vary from time to time, and on a future trip to the area, the opposite side of the blow-out may be blown clean.

Buffalo Jump and Wallow Sites

Another site worth mentioning is the so-called "buffalo jump," which is occasionally found at the base of a rather high cliff. Such a hunting or kill site is shown in illustration number 91. Buffalo were driven to the edge of a cliff to the point where they eventually pushed one another over the cliff. The buffalo were then killed or butchered at the base of the cliff. Many artifacts other than arrowheads have been found in these processing sites. Knives and scrapers will usually outnumber arrowheads. Although much has been said and written about the so-called buffalo jump sites, I have personally known of very few and suspect that they are not as numerous as commonly thought to be. A similar site, shown in illustration number 92, is the buffalo wallow, where buffalo gathered because of the perpetual presence of water, mud, or moisture. These sites are normally hunting or kill sites, although they may also be campsites. The actual site shown in the illustration is the dark area in the center foreground just below the long snow bank.

Illustration 91

A buffalo jump site shown in the center of the photograph and below the cliffs at the top.

Illustration 92

The buffalo wallow site shown in the center of the photograph and below the snowbank is in the darker soil which was heavily soaked with what appears to be perpetual moisture in an area between two springs.

Illustration 93

The campsite shown above entirely circled the promontory point or rock outcropping standing alone on the prairie. Note also the remains of a homesteader's ranch buildings around the rock formation. A natural lake exists to the right of the rock formation out of the photograph.

Industrial Sites

A common site is the industrial site, which is ordinarily found near natural flint outcroppings. In the Colorado and Wyoming foothills these sites are common. Flint materials that are native to an area are commonly located toward the tops of the ridges in natural outcroppings. Occasionally you will find an artifact at one of these sites, but more often than not, very little of the flint material will be worked. Larger pieces were normally broken down into pieces more suitable for transportation. In this respect, a thorough search of the area should be made, because a campsite may be found in the immediate vicinity. Indians ordinarily did not transport heavy rock any farther than necessary unless the material was unique and of a fine quality.

Lookout Sites

The lookout site can be easily confused with the industrial site, especially with a natural outcropping of flint nearby. Indians on a high lookout would often make arrowheads and other artifacts to pass the time. The lookout site will obviously be located on a very high area and can be distinguished from the industrial site by the presence of many more smaller-sized flakes and chips of flint resulting from pressure flaking. Percussion flaking was ordinarily used at the industrial site, and the pieces of flint material remaining will normally be larger than those left at the lookout site.

Ceremonial Sites

The ceremonial site, in my opinion, is characterized by the presence of the so-called "teepee rings," some as large as forty feet in diameter. These sites will usually be found not far from a campsite and generally on high ground, although I have seen this type of site occasionally on lower ground. It has also been my experience that artifacts in ceremonial sites are rare. Some authorities would probably dispute this finding. A ceremonial site can be easily distinguished from a campsite or industrial site because of the lack of many large or small chips or flakes of flint material.

Common Characteristics

One characteristic that seems common to almost all artifact sites is their location on high ground in comparison to the surrounding terrain. This is not always true, however, for one of the finest campsites I have ever hunted is located on a wide-open, low-lying area with several surrounding hills and ridges. The presence of an excellent spring and pond is perhaps the main reason why many different cultures of Indians used this site over literally thousands of years. Both Sandia and Folsom points have been found at this site, together with the more modern-day arrowheads of perhaps the Arapaho, Shoshone, and Ute tribes. This site, for that matter, is without question the most productive one I have ever hunted year in and year out. To show how artifacts will "work up" or "weather out" of the ground (as described more fully in Chapter 6), I found part of a Folsom point at this site in the early 1960s, and fifteen years later, my daughter found another portion of the same point in the same general area. Given enough years, we may eventually find the entire Folsom point!

Another good place to hunt for artifacts is around a promontory point, such as the rock outcropping in the center of the prairie land shown in illustration number 93. Such outcroppings seem to have attracted the Indian, perhaps for protection against the elements in temporary camping, or perhaps as a hiding place to help in hunting game animals. Such locations are not always on high ground, and, in fact, many are located in rather low areas. In any case, even one lone, unusual outcropping in the middle of a flat plain may very well have one or more artifacts in the surrounding area.

Outside of the few exceptions described above, high ground is the more likely location for most sites. I have seen areas in eastern Colorado where every high knoll on the relatively level terrain was literally covered with flint material. Also, remember that the arrowhead featured on the title page was found in the middle of Greeley, Colorado, on what used to be known as "Petrikin's Hill." This high knoll is now occupied by the student center of the University of Northern Colorado. It is hard to picture the site as once being an Indian campsite. Likewise, the highest part of Longmont, Colorado, known as Sunset Hill, was once an Indian campsite but is now occupied by a golf course and small reservoir. Pioneers of the area have found several arrowheads on the hill when it still existed as native soil. These are only two examples; there are, no doubt, many more such former sites on higher ground in cities and towns now covered by asphalt, grass, and cement that will never again yield an artifact.

The early American Indian probably camped occasionally on the banks of streams and creeks. Early fur trappers described such camps in the Rocky Mountain region in later writings and journals. I suspect, however, that many artifacts found in creekbeds and along the low-lying areas around rivers resulted from hunting rather than camping activities. Game animals frequented these areas in years gone by, and, of course, even today rivers are still considered to be good hunting areas because of the presence of water and vegetation. Similarly, old-timers have described finding many arrowheads and other stone artifacts in the low valley areas of both Carter Lake and Horsetooth Reservoir in the northern Colorado foothills back in the early 1900s before either reservoir was constructed. These areas, now totally covered with water, were probably once very good hunting grounds.

It has been said than an arrowhead or artifact can be found anywhere, and I suspect that this may be true. I have heard of arrowheads being found in graveled driveways, the gravel having been transported from gravel pits along rivers in the area. Similarly, I heard that an arrowhead was dug out of the asphalt in a Fort Collins, Colorado, city street—again probably originally carried in with the gravel from a river in the area. Other such stories are common, so I always look for artifacts wherever I am. You just never know when or where one may turn up.

Before we leave the subject, I would like to mention the best way to familiarize yourself with the general area you plan to hunt both before and during your trip. United States Geological Survey quadrangle maps, as shown in illustration number 94, are excellent for studying the topography and terrain of a given area. If you are not totally familiar with an area, they may even keep you from getting lost while hunting, for almost every dirt road and trail is shown, including many which will not be shown on an ordinary road map. Variation in elevation, including mountain tops and drainage areas, are shown together with natural and man-made landmarks, such as springs, wells, mines, lakes, quarries, and rivers. Each map covers only a given area known as a quadrangle. Some maps may cover actually more than one quadrangle in more isolated areas. Each map will be named in accordance with a well-known landmark in the area. Sometimes you can study one of these maps before a trip and actually pinpoint several possible artifact sites without ever having seen the terrain itself. These maps and a symbol chart, such as that shown in illustration number 95, are available from various U.S. Geological Survey offices throughout the country and also at certain bookstores, outdoor stores, and real estate offices.

The best way to locate a site is to be fortunate enough to have someone show you or tell you where one is. You may find a site

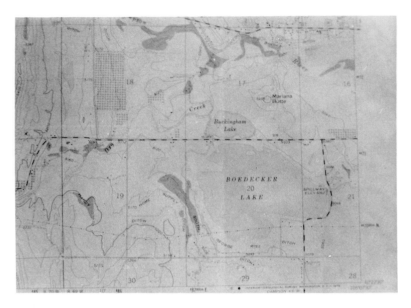

Illustration 94
United States Geological Survey map, or quadrangle map.

pretty well hunted out in this manner, but in future years, after erosive forces have affected the surface, many new artifacts may eventually show up. The arrowhead hunter's dream, of course, is to walk upon a site perhaps in an isolated area that no one has hunted for many years. These sites seem few and far between, and you may have to walk for miles and even for many years to discover one. I have personally run across very few sites such as this over the years, but the possibility is always there. This is what keeps you walking over "just one more ridge" in search of the elusive artifact.

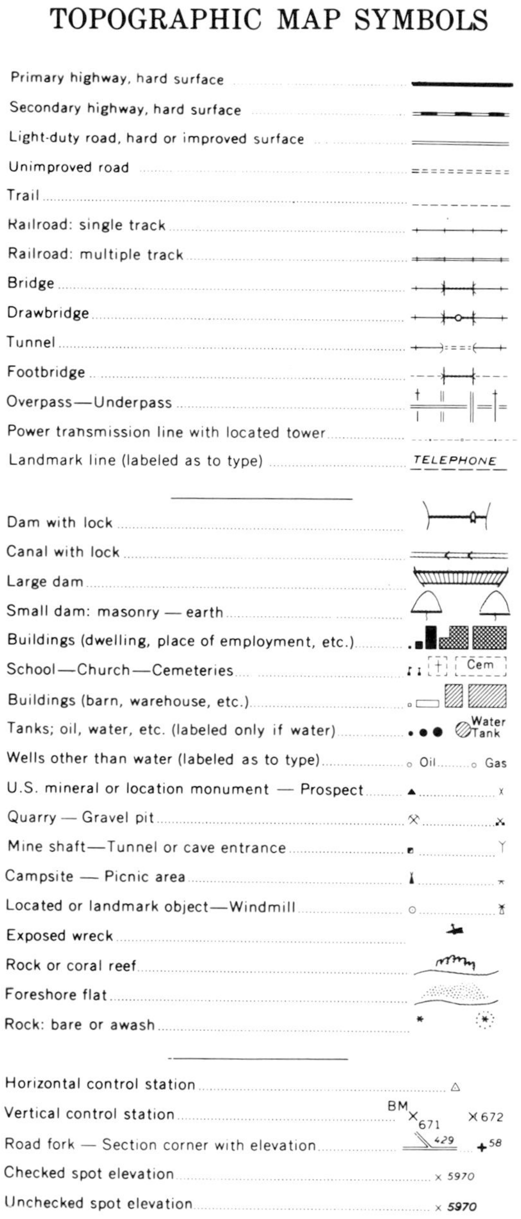

TOPOGRAPHIC MAP SYMBOLS

Primary highway, hard surface

Secondary highway, hard surface

Light-duty road, hard or improved surface

Unimproved road

Trail

Railroad: single track

Railroad: multiple track

Bridge

Drawbridge

Tunnel

Footbridge

Overpass—Underpass

Power transmission line with located tower

Landmark line (labeled as to type)   *TELEPHONE*

Dam with lock

Canal with lock

Large dam

Small dam: masonry — earth

Buildings (dwelling, place of employment, etc.)

School—Church—Cemeteries   Cem

Buildings (barn, warehouse, etc.)

Tanks; oil, water, etc. (labeled only if water)   Water Tank

Wells other than water (labeled as to type)   o Oil   o Gas

U.S. mineral or location monument — Prospect   ▲   x

Quarry — Gravel pit

Mine shaft—Tunnel or cave entrance

Campsite — Picnic area

Located or landmark object—Windmill   o

Exposed wreck

Rock or coral reef

Foreshore flat

Rock: bare or awash   *

Horizontal control station   △

Vertical control station   BM ×₆₇₁   X 672

Road fork — Section corner with elevation   429   +58

Checked spot elevation   x 5970

Unchecked spot elevation   x *5970*

Illustration 95

Geological Survey map symbol chart.

VARIATIONS WILL BE FOUND ON OLDER MAPS

Boundary: national

State

county, parish, municipio

civil township, precinct, town, barrio

incorporated city, village, town, hamlet

reservation, national or state

small park, cemetery, airport, etc.

land grant

Township or range line, U.S. land survey

Section line, U.S. land survey

Township line, not U.S. land survey

Section line, not U.S. land survey

Fence line or field line

Section corner: found—indicated

Boundary monument: land grant—other

Index contour   Intermediate contour

Supplementary cont.   Depression contours

Cut — Fill   Levee

Mine dump   Large wash

Dune area   Tailings pond

Sand area   Distorted surface

Tailings   Gravel beach

Glacier   Intermittent streams

Perennial streams   Aqueduct tunnel

Water well—Spring   Falls

Rapids   Intermittent lake

Channel   Small wash

Sounding—Depth curve   Marsh (swamp)

Dry lake bed   Land subject to controlled inundation

Woodland   Mangrove

Submerged marsh   Scrub

Orchard   Wooded marsh

Vineyard   Bldg. omission area

Illustration 95 (continued)
Geological Survey map symbol chart.

Illustration 96

Arrowhead to the left of center in the photograph was uncovered by a rain in a heavy clay soil.

CHAPTER 6

HOW TO
HUNT ARTIFACTS

Once you know what to look for and where to look, it helps considerably to know how to hunt stone artifacts. Every artifact collector has his or her own style and method of hunting artifacts. Those that follow are my own and have proven productive over a period of thirty years.

In my part of the country, I tend to hunt the lower elevations from October to April in order to avoid the rattlesnake season at elevations less than six thousand feet. I have encountered very few rattlesnakes in summer hunting at lower elevations, but the possibility is always present. When you have to concentrate on trying to avoid rattlesnakes, it seriously breaks the concentration required to find artifacts. I would prefer not to have to worry about rattlesnakes at all. During the snake season, therefore, I hunt from April to October in the higher mountain elevations above six thousand feet. Hunting the higher elevations during these months also seems to coincide with more favorable weather conditions at higher elevations in the summer and lower elevations in the winter. Also, as long as snow does not completely cover the ground, it is possible to hunt artifacts through the winter at lower elevations.

I also have a pattern of hunting various sites at certain times of the year. Some sites are good enough that a yearly visit will yield several new artifacts on the surface that have weathered up from rains and winds over the past year. Sometimes after a hard summer cloudburst, a site may have several new artifacts washed up more often than yearly. Good hunting at these sites may exist several times a year. Sites this good, however, are rare. The constant forces of erosion have to be taken into account wherever you are looking for artifacts.

In northern Colorado and southern Wyoming, for instance, artifacts will work up to the surface in both the mountains and plains through heaving of the soil caused by intermittent freezing and thawing. In sandy or sandy loam soil areas generally in the plains, most artifacts will work up through heavy winds blowing the topsoil. In foothill or mountain areas predominantly of clay soils or hard rocky ground, most artifacts will work up by heavy rains washing an area clean. Wind does not move much of the topsoil in this type of area and therefore plays a very small role in weathering up artifacts. On the other hand, water will erode topsoil in sandy plains areas as much as wind, especially in areas that are not level. It pays to be aware of recent weather conditions in the area you plan to hunt. Illustration numbers 96 through 101 show various arrowheads in situ which have been uncovered either by wind or rain. Note the texture of the surrounding ground in each photograph.

I like to hunt in direct sunlight, preferably walking directly into the sun. This way I do not cast a shadow ahead of myself. An artifact is much harder to spot in a shadow than directly in the sun. Walking into the sun will actually cause an artifact to be visible from up to thirty feet away. In this regard, I never hunt artifacts while wearing sunglasses, since they take away the shine of the flint material. With the sun high overhead, I have found far more artifacts around midday than in the early morning or later afternoon hours, when the angle of the sun is such that very strange shadows are cast by vegetation, including the smallest clumps of grass.

While walking over an area, there are certain features, both natural and unnatural, to look for. I have found a great number of artifacts in man-made dirt roads and trails made by livestock and game animals. These areas are normally barren and, of course, are subject to constant wearing away of the soil by forces other than nature. Many of these roads and trails will pass right through campsites, and flint material will be much more readily visible than in the surrounding rougher, grassy terrain. Walking is easier and traveling is faster on these roads and trails, and your

Illustration 97
The white arrowhead in this photograph was exposed by strong winds blowing a light loam soil.

chances of walking into a site are just as good as simply meandering through an area.

In this connection, any area that has been pulverized by cattle or sheep is worth examining. Livestock will bed down for the night in protected areas such as where an Indian campsite may have been located in years gone by. Livestock will also frequent a spring or pond area where a campsite may have been located. These animals will constantly keep the topsoil stirred up and aid in the working up of artifacts. I have found many arrowheads on ground literally churned up and half covered with manure. Similarly, I have found many good campsites near old ranch buildings and corrals. The reason for this is fairly obvious. The homesteader generally built ranch houses and livestock facilities near springs or creeks in exactly the same areas that Indians occupied because of the proximity of water. It is easy to overlook the potential of these areas while passing through or obtaining permission to hunt nearby lands.

Illustration 98

Arrowhead in the lower center of the photograph was uncovered by rain washing through grass on a heavier soil almost totally granite covered.

Illustration 99

Arrowhead exposed by rain and washed up in a rocky, heavier soil.

Illustration 100

Arrowhead to the left center of photograph was uncovered by wind blowing a light sandy soil in an area of sparse vegetation.

Likewise, an area with a large prairie dog colony may be worth examining. These animals will also literally churn up the soil and uncover a surprising number of artifacts. This is especially true if you are hunting at a known site. My favorite campsite on the Colorado-Wyoming border is almost totally covered by two large separate prairie dog colonies. The prairie dogs have the same effect as a plow and constantly churn up artifacts at this site. My daughter found three arrowheads in less than forty-five seconds on the surface of dirt excavated by a prairie dog from one individual prairie dog hole. As a word of precaution, however, be very careful not to reach into a prairie dog hole and take the chance of being bitten by an animal that may carry rabies. Also, in a large colony of prairie dogs, be careful where you walk. The widespread underground tunneling by the prairie dog can cause an area to be susceptible to surface collapse. Furthermore, at lower elevations, a prairie dog hole is a good place to find a rattlesnake during the snake season.

In hunting artifacts, travel as lightly as possible. Depending

Illustration 101

The arrowhead to the left and below center of the photograph (at the right side of larger rock) was probably washed out of totally rocky ground or perhaps may have always remained fully exposed over the years.

upon weather conditions, usually all you need are a hat for protection from the sun, a good jacket with sufficient pockets, a good pair of high-top boots, possibly a pair of gloves, a canteen, a camera, a pocket knife, matches, occasionally a compass, a small first-aid kit, a Geological Survey map of the area, and perhaps a small quantity of food, depending on how long you plan to hunt and how far away from your car you plan to get. Some of these standard hunting accessories are shown in illustration number 102. I always try to leave extra pocket space for artifacts and use a small coin purse for arrowheads, since a bag or container is cumbersome to carry. Also, a carpenter's nail apron may be tied around your waist and used easily. It doesn't take very many grinding stones to weight a person down pretty fast. Some people like to carry a broom handle with a nail in the end of it or a long-handled dandelion digger for turning flint on the ground without bending over. In recent years I have begun using such a hunting stick, and in an area covered with flint, it definitely saves both time and wear and tear on the lower back!

Illustration 102

Typical arrowhead hunting gear consisting of binoculars, hunting stick, camera,
canteen, map, coin purse, pocket knife, and compass.

Such a hunting stick can also be used to poke around through
the sand under a rock overhang. The Indian frequently sought
temporary shelter under a rock overhang where there was
protection from the weather. Many nice stone artifacts have
been found in sandy areas immediately below or under such
overhangs. These areas should only be excavated by the
professional archaeologist and any disturbance of the ground
should be kept to a minimum—simply poking through the sand
rather than digging. Excavation is hard work and disruptive to the
natural terrain and should be left to the professional. I prefer
surface hunting only and actually enjoy waiting for artifacts to
weather up to the surface.

One final rule of thumb for hunting artifacts should be
mentioned. Whenever you find simply a piece of an artifact,
always remember to scan the immediate area for several feet and
look for the other part that has broken off. If the break in the
artifact is clean or straight, there is a good chance it may have
happened in recent years, many times by livestock stepping on

the artifact. The other piece may be but a few feet away on the surface of the ground. On the other hand, if the break is uneven or shattered, it probably happened upon original impact (in the case of an arrowhead) years or centuries ago and chances are remote that the remaining part can be found. Even if you cannot find the remaining piece, remember the exact area and prepare a site map. Years later you may be able to go back and find the remaining part of the artifact when it has weathered up to the surface.

In hunting artifacts, always look for pictographs and petroglyphs on rock walls and smooth stone surfaces. Petroglyphs are figures incised, scored, or pecked into the surface of the stone, while pictographs are painted figures. Pictographs will ordinarily only be found in caves or places protected extremely well from the weather. Petroglyphs, on the other hand, while certainly not invincible to the elements, will withstand weather conditions over many more years. Illustration number 103 shows some petroglyphs found in southern

Illustration 103
Petroglyphs on a rock wall or overhang. Note vandalism by modern man seriously detracting from the ancient art.

Illustration 104

Except for the buffalo horn and rattlesnake rattles, this photograph consists entirely of assorted modern man-made items that can also be found frequently while hunting stone artifacts.

Wyoming. While they have withstood the forces of nature, man has managed to disfigure the original designs, which is certainly tragic to anyone with even the slightest conscience!

While hunting artifacts, you may also find many other interesting items from bygone years, both natural and man-made. Some examples are shown in illustration numbers 104 and 105. I have accumulated buffalo horns, deer horns, bighorn sheep horns, horseshoes, rattlesnake rattles, old gun shell casings, including buffalo gun cartridges, antique barbed wire and nails, and old coins. Some people have even found antique guns, cowboy spurs, and oxen shoes, which are far more scarce than horseshoes. Also, if you are generally a rockhound as I am, you can find many interesting rock and shell specimens, such as those shown in illustration number 105. One that comes to mind is the so-called "desert rose," which I have only found in one specific area along the Colorado-Wyoming border. A desert rose is shown at the left end of the center row in illustration number

105. Fossils are also frequently found, together with petrified bones and sea shells. Anyone with a general interest in nature can also observe wildlife and merely enjoy just getting out for a little fresh air.

Illustration 105

Miscellaneous stone items, shown above, include (bottom row left to right): whetstone, perforated disc, shell fossil, petrified fish or aquatic animal; (center row, left to right): desert rose, quartz crystal, sea shells, fossilized sea shell, petrified jawbone containing teeth; (top row, left to right): perforated disc, clay pottery, shell fossil, cup or bowl with round stone ball.

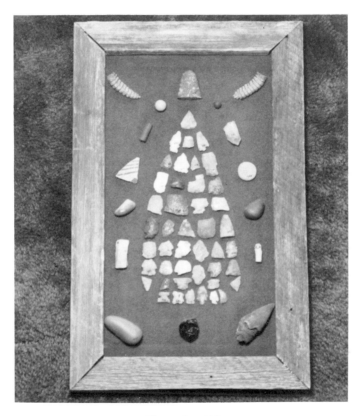

Illustration 106
Arrowhead design frame, also containing interesting miscellaneous finds.

CHAPTER 7

WHAT TO DO WITH A COLLECTION

Over the years, many outstanding artifact collections have wound up hidden in attic trunks, basement boxes, and coffee cans—often in the possession of someone who had inherited them and who also could care less what they were, where they came from, and where they were going to end up. In my opinion, this is tragic—artifacts perhaps thousands of years old simply being ignored, neglected, and forgotten while all the attention is given to a rusty milk can probably less than fifty years old. The true antiquity is ignored, giving way to the so-called "antique" butter churn. The artifacts more often than not end up under the auctioneer's gavel with all the old bushel baskets, Mason jars, and broken picture frames. It is a tragedy that the true antiques that were collected in the old sheepherder's tobacco can are given such a stately funeral at a rummage sale, but this is all too often the case.

It would seem to me that the average person might be a bit more interested in the history of man through the ages and at least see to it that artifact collections are given to the local museum where they belong if no one else is interested enough to preserve and perhaps display them. Many artifacts have, of course, ended up with the local museum, but all too often this is not the case. In my opinion, an artifact worth keeping is an artifact worth displaying. This means that all artifacts can and should be not only preserved, but also displayed.

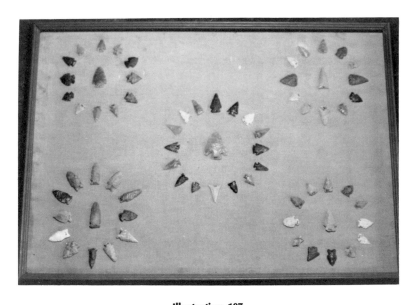

Illustration 107

Arrowhead frame containing some of the better arrowheads in the author's family collection.

There are many ways you can display artifacts. Picture frame designs for wall mounting are probably the most common. With this method, there is practically no limit to the number of designs that can be used. Even broken arrowheads and other artifacts can be arranged in attractive eye-catching designs. See illustration number 106 for a good example of how to arrange and display broken artifacts. I typically find at least ten broken artifacts for each whole or perfect artifact, so there are always plenty of broken artifacts that can be arranged in a number of designs. Perfect arrowheads, of course, make very attractive frames for wall hanging, as well as knives, scrapers, drills, and awls. A frame containing perfect arrowheads is shown in illustration number 107. I have made several frames from old gray weathered lumber. I prefer these over frames purchased in stores. On the other hand, frames or shadow boxes that make very attractive artifact displays can be purchased. Shadow boxes, which are glassed-in, also are about the only safe way to publicly display artifacts. Other artifact display frames are shown in illustration number 108.

Illustration 108
Assorted artifact frames in author's family collection.

The larger, heavier artifacts such as grinding stones and grinding slabs are ordinarily not suitable for framing and wall hanging. These artifacts can be displayed nicely in regular or glassed-in bookshelves. Glassed-in frames or boxes are also appropriate for table-top display and with careful workmanship can be made suitable for wall hanging.

One decision that has to be made is whether or not the artifact should be cleaned and/or polished prior to mounting or framing. I prefer to wash my artifacts with a solution of warm water and dishwashing soap. An old toothbrush does as good a job as anything to help remove soil and mineral stains and bring out the natural beauty of the flint material. It is surprising how discolored a beautiful piece of flint can become after lying in the ground for hundreds of years. The toothbrush ordinarily does a good job of getting the discoloration or dirt out of the small cracks and crevices created during the original flaking of the artifact.

On the other hand, the natural aging process known as patination is a condition whereby minerals in the soil actually build up or accumulate on the surface of the artifact over many hundreds or thousands of years. This patination, in essence, almost becomes a part of the artifact itself and is very difficult, if not impossible, to remove with a toothbrush and soapy water. You almost have to scrape off patination with a pocketknife or blade. When attempting this, it is easy to permanently damage the surface of the artifact. For this reason, I never attempt to remove patination. Furthermore, the archaeological value of the artifact may be lost by removing patination, since it usually indicates a more ancient artifact. An artifact completely "encased" by patination is a rare find and, in my opinion, is nice to mount and display "as is." Some collectors prefer to polish artifacts prior to display. I have never done this and probably never will. Polishing seems to create an unnatural appearance, and I simply do not prefer to "dress-up" the collection to this extent.

Aside from display of artifacts, **every collector should catalog the location of each artifact that he or she finds.** This can be done on U.S. Geological Survey maps, although in small areas where several artifacts are found, you may have to draw a site map to show exact location of a great number of artifacts in a small area. Cataloging and mapping may seem unnecessary at first when your overall number of artifacts is small, but as time goes by and the number of artifacts increases, it is next to impossible to remember exactly where you have found every artifact. As a general scientific proposition, much can also be learned from relative location of artifacts in the field at the site location.

In cataloging and mapping, it is mandatory that each artifact be numbered and dated as to when it was found. Otherwise, it is easy to mix-up and confuse one similar artifact with another. **Artifacts should be cataloged as to date found, color, type, location, and flint material.** Cataloging and mapping, together with site photography, are a very important prerequisite to scientific archaeology and have always been one dividing line between amateur and professional archaeologists. Perhaps if the amateur archaeologist or collector were more careful with this aspect of collecting, he or she would command more respect from the professional archaeolgoist and may even escape the label "pot hunter."

As a collection grows and gains in prominence and respectability, the day may come when public display might be appropriate. A museum, of course, is the most appropriate place

Illustration 109
Large arrowhead found by the author in 1980 shown in actual size.

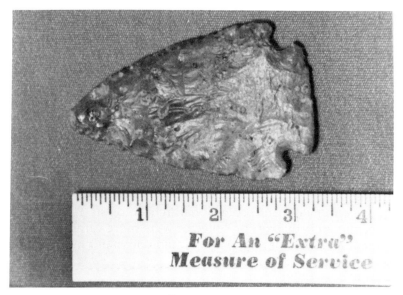

Illustration 110
Spearpoint found in 1982 in southern Wyoming by Mrs. Judy Wood of Loveland, Colorado.

for public display and for future preservation. It may even keep the artifacts off the auction block! Other than museums and occasional store window display, artifact shows are probably the only other chance for public display of artifacts. One such show is held annually in September at Loveland, Colorado, and is known as the Loveland Stone Age Fair. This event is supervised by the Loveland Archaeological Society, Inc. and is most worthwhile and educational. Collectors from throughout the United States have displayed artifacts at this fair, which originated in 1934 when it was first held at Cornish, Colorado.

You can also join the local chapter of your state archaeological society to gain further knowledge of archaeology and to expand and further define your artifact collection. Through research, comparing, exchange of ideas, and field trips, much knowledge can be gained and passed on to further archaeological study for future generations.

A very interesting and unique program is currently being conducted through the Office of the State Archaeologist of the state of Colorado in Denver. This is the Program for Avocational Archaeological Certification, otherwise known as the PAAC Survey Program. This program consists of a series of courses on Anthropology and Archaeology and related scientific aspects, including dating methods. Site survey and laboratory analysis are also covered in the program, together with fieldwork procedures. This new program does appear to be very worthwhile and educational and may go a long way toward bringing amateur and professional archaeologists into closer harmony and cooperation.

Please remember that if, in your own artifact hunting, you discover a truly unique site or very unusual artifact, you should notify the Office of your State Archaeologist where site records are maintained. In Colorado, this office is located in the Colorado Historical Society Museum in Denver. Over the years, amateur archaeologists have made significant contributions to our knowledge of prehistory.

Finally, to show that beautiful arrowheads can still be found, illustration numbers 109 and 110 show two arrowheads found since I began writing this book. The large white arrowhead shown in illustration number 109 was found by me on Labor Day 1980 in southern Wyoming. The large spearpoint shown in illustration number 110 was found by Mrs. Judy Wood of Loveland, Colorado, also in southern Wyoming in the spring of

1982. This arrowhead in particular is a truly amazing find and one which shows us there will always be one more arrowhead to find—somewhere, sometime!

Illustration 111
Now . . . can you find an arrowhead in this picture?

Illustration 112
Grandchildren Katie and Nicole holding an arrowhead found by Nicole in 1985.

BIBLIOGRAPHY

Benson, Laurel. *Colorado From Indians to Industry* (Loveland, Colorado: Center for In-Service Education, Inc., 1975).

Bradford, George. *Paleo Points, Volume One* (Ontario, Canada: George R. Bradford, 1976).

Brennan, Louis A. *Beginner's Guide to Archaeology* (Harrisburg, Pennsylvania: The Stackpole Company, 1973).

Celoria, Francis. *Archaeology* (New York: Bantam, 1973).

Chesterman, Charles W. *The Audubon Society Field Guide to North American Rocks and Minerals* (New York: Alfred A. Knopf, Inc., 1978).

Encyclopedia Brittanica, Inc. *Encyclopedia Brittanica* (Chicago, Illinois: William Benton, 1970).

Haynes, Vance, and Agogino, George. *Geological Significance of a New Radiocarbon Date from the Lindenmeier Site* (Denver, Colorado: The Denver Museum of Natural History, 1960).

Hibben, Frank C. *The Lost Americans* (New York: Thomas Y. Crowell Company, 1946, 1968).

Hibben, Frank C. *Digging Up America* (New York: Hill and Wang, 1960).

Hothem, Lar. *North American Indian Artifacts* (Florence, Alabama: Books Americana, Inc., 1978).

150   Arrowheads and Stone Artifacts

Hughes, J. Donald. *American Indians in Colorado* (Boulder, Colorado: Pruett Publishing Company, 1977).

Irwin, H.J., and Irwin, C.C. *Excavations at the Lo Dais Ka Site in the Denver, Colorado, Area* (Denver, Colorado: The Denver Museum of Natural History, 1959).

Irwin-Williams, Cynthia, and Irwin, Henry J. *Excavations at Magic Mountain* (Denver, Colorado: The Denver Museum of Natural History, 1966).

Look, Al. *1,000 Million Years on the Colorado Plateau, Land of Uranium* (Denver, Colorado: Bell Publications, 1955).

Murray, Robert A. *Pipestone, A History* (Minn.: The Pipestone Indian Shrine Association and National Park Service, United States Department of Interior, 1965).

Murray, Robert A. *Pipes on the Plains* (Minn.: The Pipestone Indian Shrine Association and National Park Service, United States Department of Interior, 1968, 1975).

Robbins, Maurice, and Irving, Mary B. *The Amateur Archaeologist's Handbook* (New York: Thomas Y. Crowell Company, 1965, 1973).

Rogers, Malcom J. *Ancient Hunters of the Far West* (San Diego, California: The Union-Tribune Publishing Company, 1966).

Ronen, Avraham. *Introducing Prehistory* (London: Cassell & Company, Ltd., 1975).

Russell, Osborne, Edited by Aubrey L. Haines. *Journal of a Trapper (1834-1843)* (Oregon Historical Society: Lincoln & London: University of Nebraska Press, A Bison Book Edition, 1955, 1965).

Russell, Virgil Y. *Indian Artifacts* (Boulder, Colorado: Johnson Publishing Company, 1951, 1957, 1962).

St. Vrain Valley Historical Association. *They Came To Stay* (Longmont, Colorado: St. Vrain Historical Society, Inc., 1971).

Steege, Louis C., and Welch, Warren W. *Stone Artifacts of the Northwestern Plains* (Colorado Springs, Colorado: Northwestern Plains Publishing Company, 1961).

United States Government. *Antiquities Act* (Washington, D.C.: 16 United States Code Annotated, Sections 431, 432, and 433).

Watson, Don. *Indians of the Mesa Verde* (Mesa Verde National Park, Colorado: Mesa Verde Museum Association, 1961).

Willey, Gordon R. *An Introduction to American Archaeology, Volume I* (Englewood Cliffs, New Jersey: Prentice-Hall, 1966).

Wormington, H.M. *Ancient Man in North America* (Denver, Colorado: The Denver Museum of Natural History, 1957).

Wormington, H.M., and Forbis, Richard G. *An Introduction to the Archaeology of Alberta, Canada* (Denver, Colorado: The Denver Museum of Natural History, 1965).

Zim, Herbert S., Shaffer, Paul R., and Perlman, Raymond. *Rocks and Minerals* (New York: Golden Press, Inc., 1957).

Index